THE Classical Guitar COMPENDIUM

Audio Access Included

Classical Masterpieces Arranged for Solo Guitar

By BRIDGET MERMIKIDES

ISBN 978-1-4803-2856-3

7777 W. BLUEMOUND RD. P.O. BOX 13819 MILWAUKEE, WI 53213

In Australia Contact:
Hal Leonard Australia Pty. Ltd.
4 Lentara Court
Cheltenham, Victoria, 3192 Australia
Email: ausadmin@halleonard.com.au

Visit Hal Leonard Online at
www.halleonard.com

For Chloe

All arrangements and performances by Bridget Mermikides.
Audio production and engineering by Milton Mermikides.

Introduction

The guitar is a relative newcomer to the family of "classical" instruments, and so its repertoire has relied on a limited amount of original works written since the 19th century, or arrangements of works for other instruments. However, as beautiful the sound of a classical guitar is, the challenge to arrange for it effectively can be tricky. A solo arrangement which is playable and preserves the musical integrity of the original work can be difficult to achieve and hard to find. This book represents years of careful work, making popular classical masterpieces work on the instrument I love. Some of these works are technically challenging so remember to stay patient and enjoy your practice as much as performing.

In addition to these 31 arrangements, I've also selected 8 studies from the classical guitar pedagogical repertoire that together provide the tools to build a really solid technical foundation. Preceding each study, I have written a set of short but important technical exercises that focus on the main challenges of the study, as well as improving general technique. These would work well as part of a daily practice and warm up regime to maintain and improve your technique.

I hope you enjoy playing these arrangements as much as I do, and they help to give you a lifetime of challenge and enjoyment with this beautiful instrument.

Bridget

Contents

Technical Studies

Although classical guitar technique is a life long study, much of it can be broken down into a series of fundamental skills, which include free stroke, rest stroke, planting, arpeggios, slurs and two part playing. In order to address these core techniques I've selected 8 studies from the classical guitar repertoire and preceded each with a set of specifically designed exercises. These exercises and studies may be used as excellent tools in your daily warm up and practice schedule.

When plucking a string remember that quality of attack and tone is all-important. There should be a point of contact with both the nail and flesh of the finger on the string and the pluck is a 'push' slightly inwards of the string by the fingertip. When the string is released the trajectory of the fingertip should follow through underneath the hand (free stroke) or it should push through to land on the next string (rest stroke).
The nails will need to be shaped and filed properly to achieve a good tone – filing in contour with the tip of the finger is a good start.

The left hand fingers need to be slightly spaced apart and should maintain a strong curve with the fingertips close to the strings. When executing a slur (hammer-on) keep the finger curved off the string as well as on and move the finger from the knuckle joint. Relax between weight and effort of the left hand and arm and do not force if aching or pain occurs. Regular focused and patient practice is the best way to develop strength and stamina.

Remember not to push the tempo beyond that which you can effectively control. If some of these tempi are beyond you, don't force it, you will get the most benefit from working at a comfortable speed and really focusing on improving the precision, tone, efficiency and relaxation in your playing. Gradually increase the tempi, over months if necessary, and never sacrifice quality of playing for the sake of speed.

The accompanying audio examples demonstrate each of these exercises at relevant tempi as well as performances of the studies, which you can use as reference tracks or even as training tools to play along to in your practice.

Sor Study No. 6 Technical Exercise

This continuous right hand free stroke exercise involves the thumb, index and middle fingers and is played at the two indicated tempi. Plant the right hand fingers on the strings as shown for stability and work to create a good quality and consistent tone on every note.

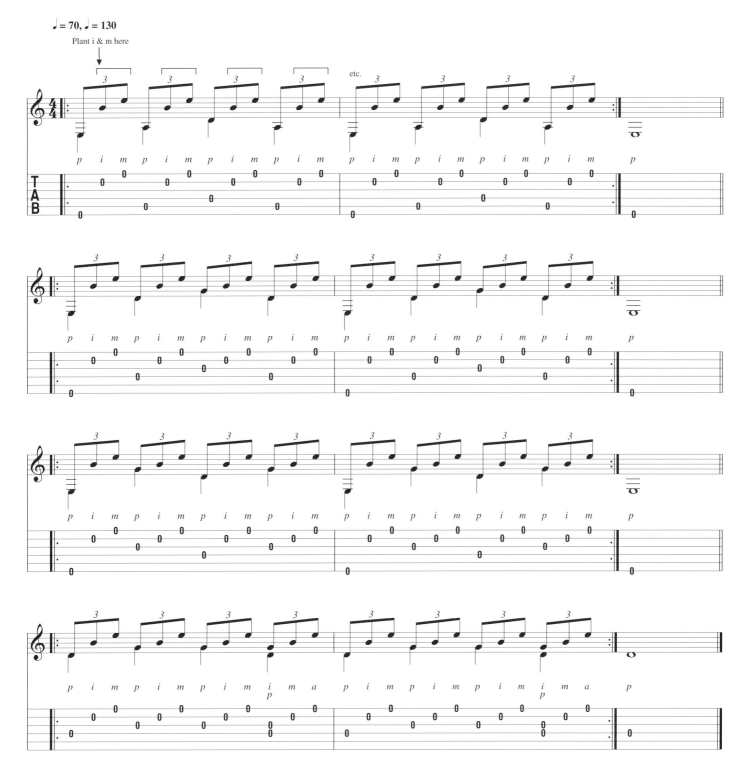

Sor Study No. 6

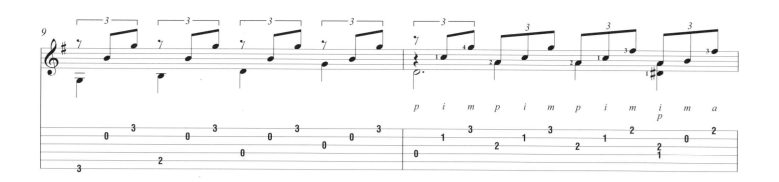

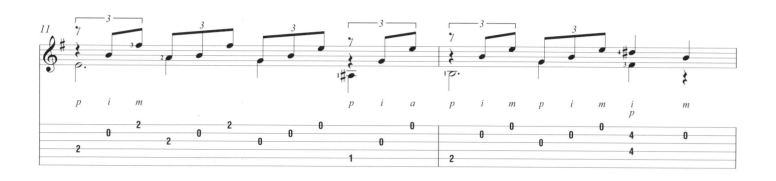

Tárrega Study in E minor Technical Exercises

This exercise combines rest stroke annular finger, with free stroke thumb index and middle fingers. This is in preparation for emphasising the annular finger melody with triplet accompaniment.

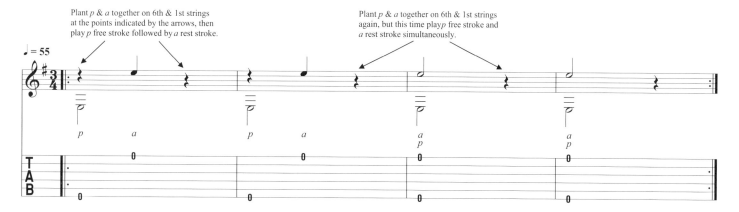

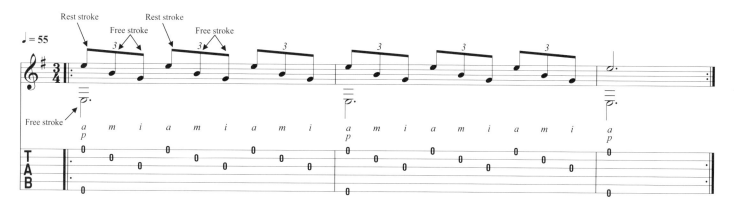

Tárrega Study in E minor

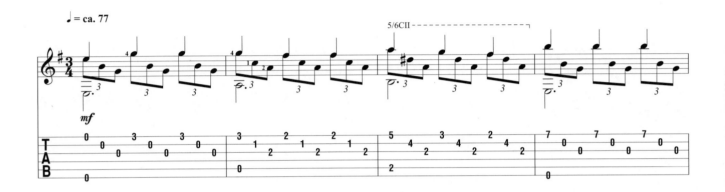

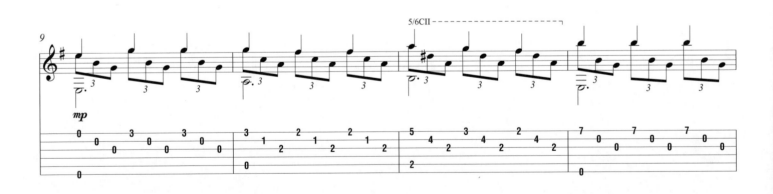

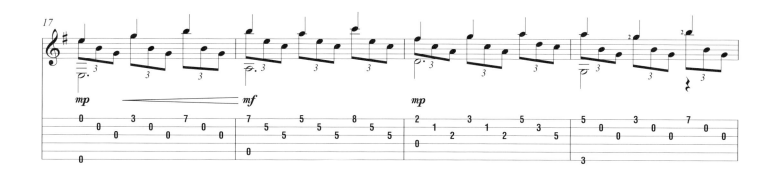

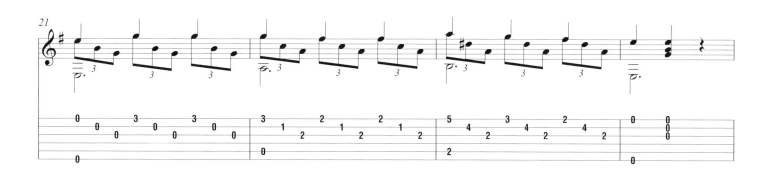

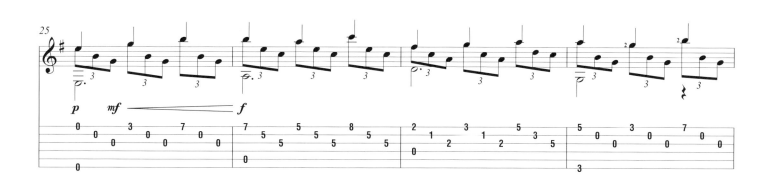

Giuliani Allegro Technical Exercises

These free stroke arpeggio exercises involve planting the fingers and thumb in precise places as indicated. When practiced correctly this will help to improve stability and security of the right hand. Work on good quality of tone throughout.

*Metronome ticks 8th notes.

*Metronome ticks 8th notes.

*Metronome ticks 8th notes.

Giuliani Allegro

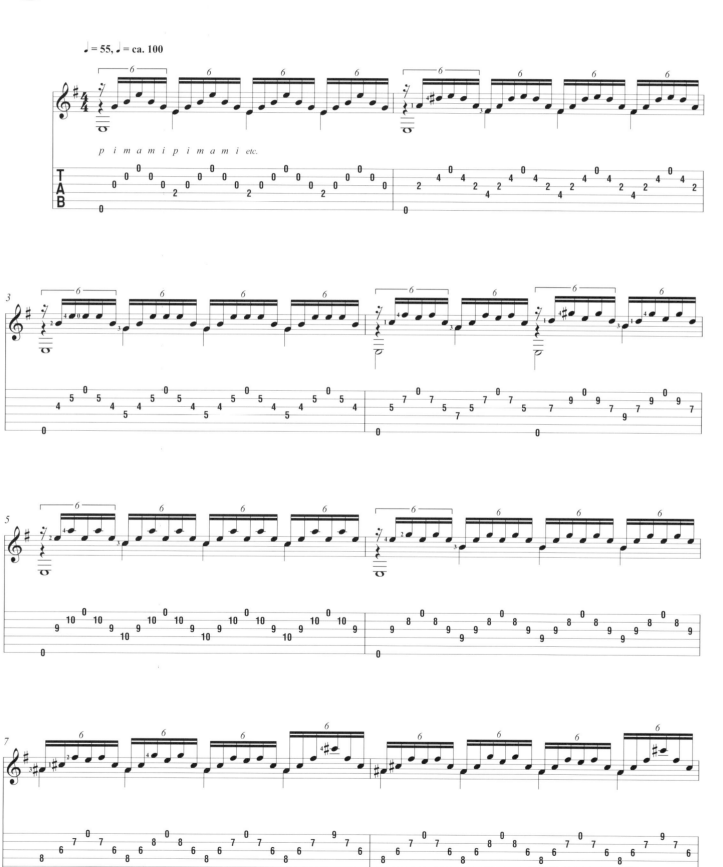

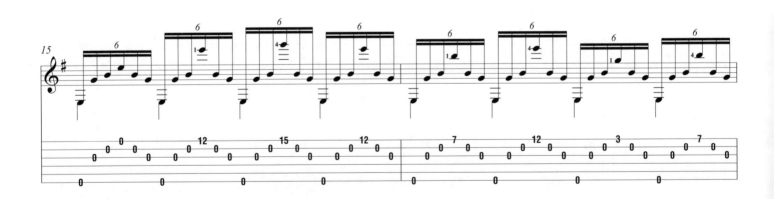

Carcassi Study No. 10 Technical Exercises

These exercises focus on left-hand slurs (hammer-ons and pull-offs). Hold down the left-hand fingers as indicated by the dashed lines and maintain a curved shape with the hammering finger both on and off the string. Each exercise is played at both slow and fast tempos.

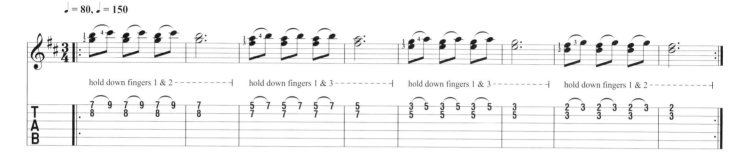

Carcassi Study No. 10

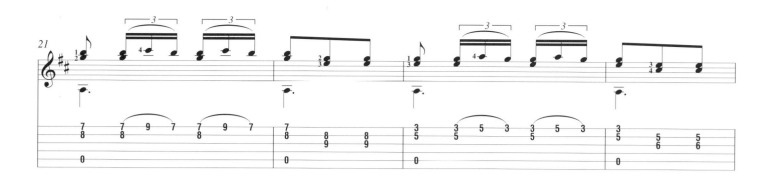

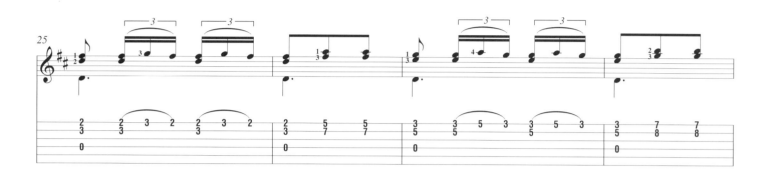

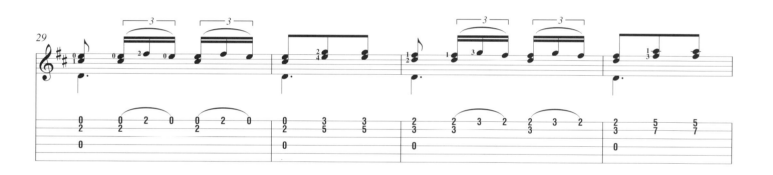

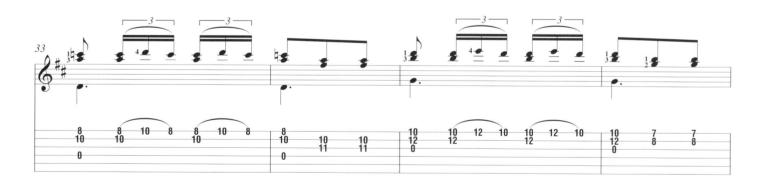

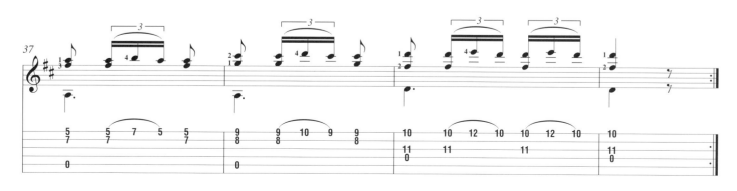

Sor Study No. 3 Technical Exercises

The first exercise below is an example of block chords followed by rests. Mute the strings by planting down the right hand fingertips on the strings and releasing left hand finger pressure simultaneously. In the second example, place down the relevant left hand fingers on the string together before executing the pull-offs. For the third example, perform the hammer-ons using finger movement from the knuckles; avoid excessive wrist or arm movement.

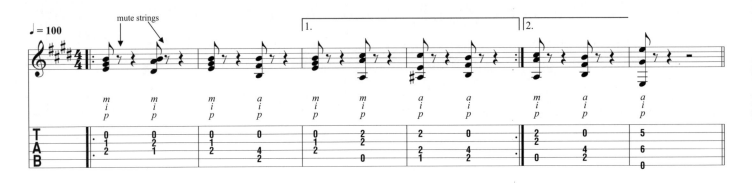

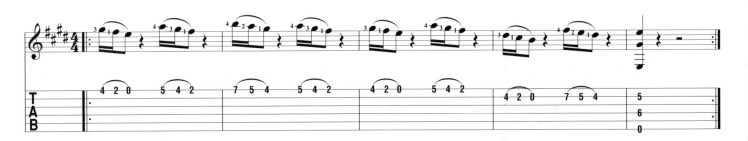

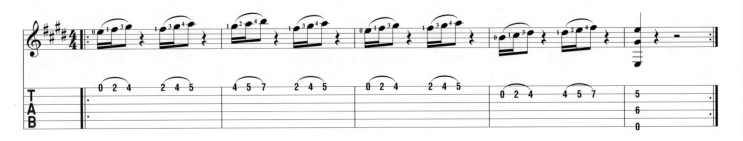

Sor Study No. 3

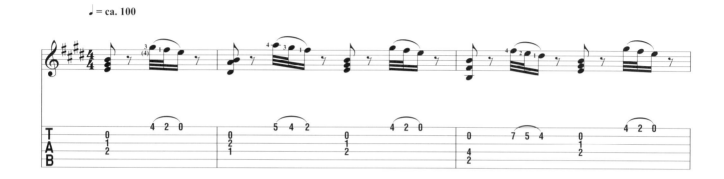

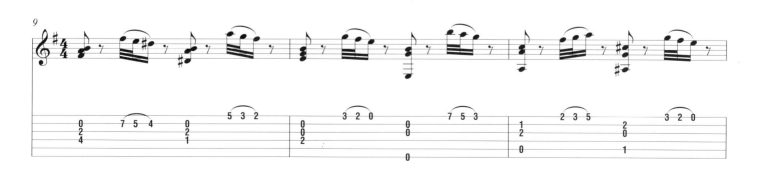

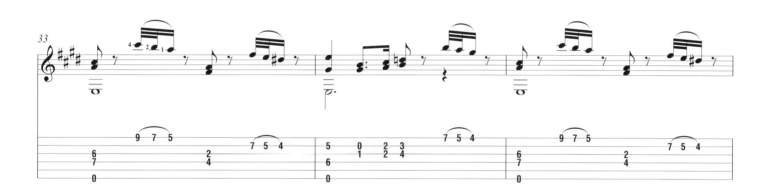

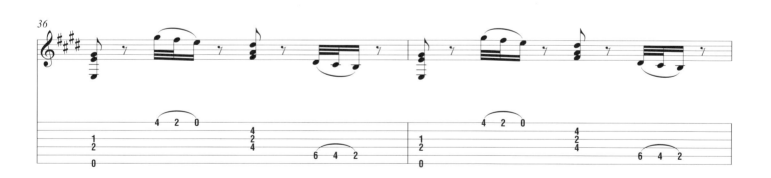

Carcassi Study No. 6 Technical Exercises

The following exercises focus on two-part playing. Play free stroke with the thumb and rest stroke with the fingers where possible and make sure the 2 beat notes sustain for their correct value.

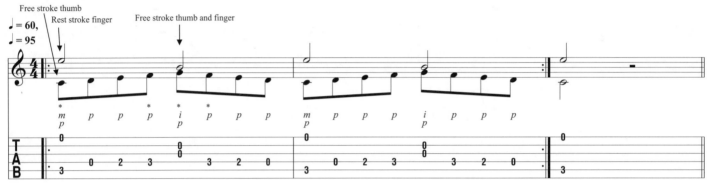

*Do not allow bass notes to over-ring when changing strings.

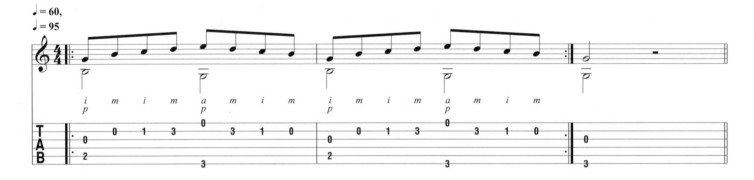

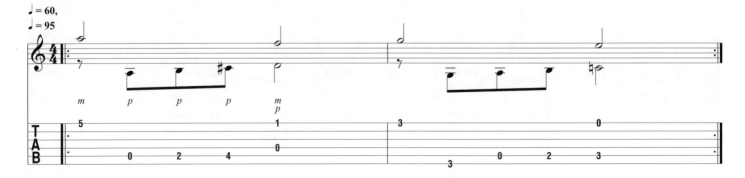

Carcassi Study No. 6

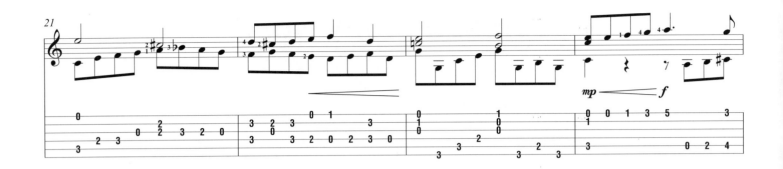

Aguado Study in D Technical Exercises

These exercises highlight slurs, arpeggios, and scale techniques.

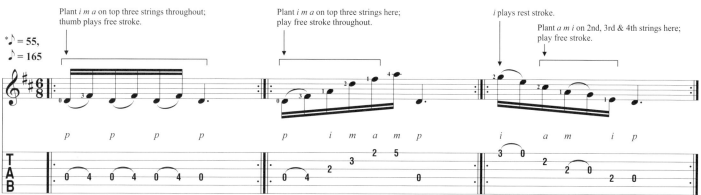

*Metronome ticks in 16th notes for tempo of ♪ = 55.

*Metronome ticks in 16th notes for tempo of ♪ = 55.

Aguado Study in D

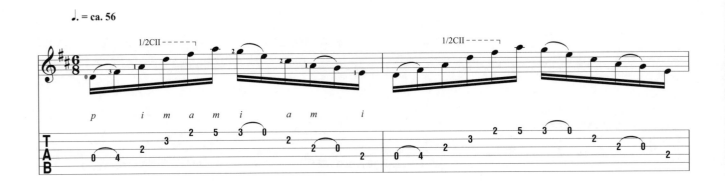

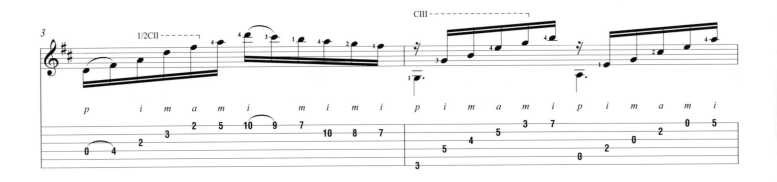

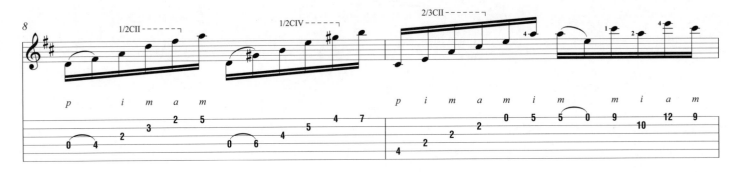

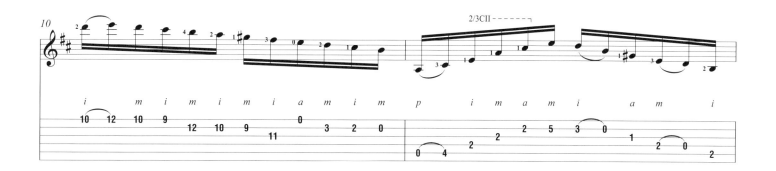

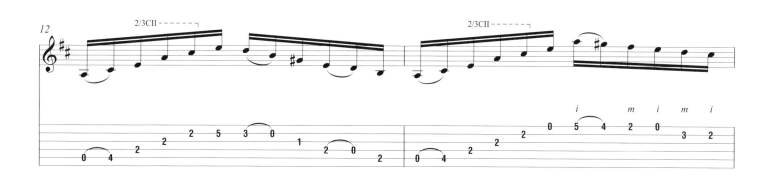

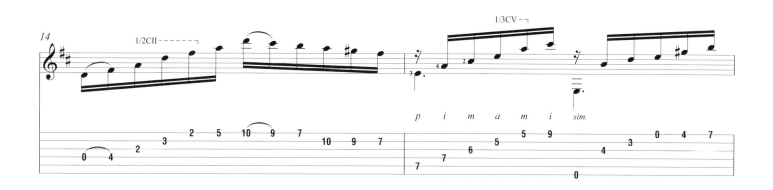

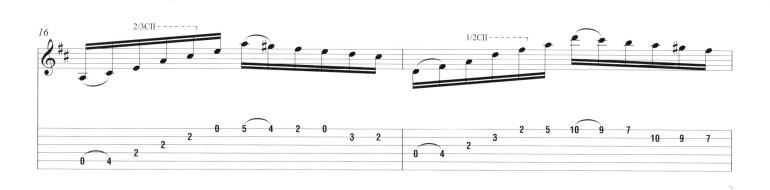

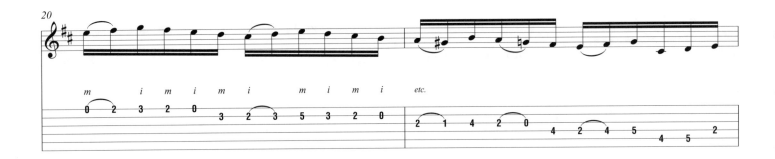

Carcassi Study No. 7 Technical Exercises

These exercises break down and separate the main technical components of Carcassi Study No. 7. Mastering these techniques individually will help to achieve a fluid performance.

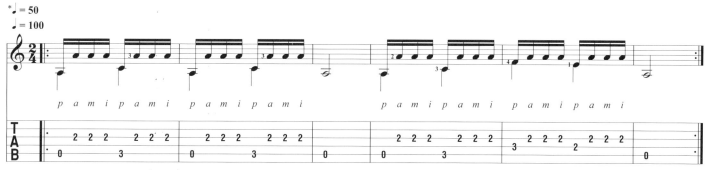

*Metronome ticks 8th notes for tempo of ♩ = 50.

This next example demonstrates arpeggio picking. Stick to using *i m* & *a* on the 3rd, 2nd and 1st strings respectively. Use the planting method for each set of four eighth notes.

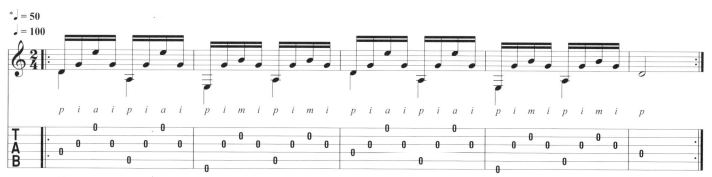

*Metronome ticks 8th notes for tempo of ♩ = 50.

The index and middle fingers in the example below alternate rest strokes with left-hand pull-offs. This technique relates to the phrases beginning in bar 16 of the Carcassi study.

*Metronome ticks 8th notes for tempo of ♩ = 50.

The last exercise alternates between thumb and middle finger free strokes, and occurs halfway through bar 17 of the Carcassi study. This technique can also be executed with the thumb and index finger.

*Metronome ticks 8th notes for tempo of ♩ = 50.

Carcassi Study No. 7

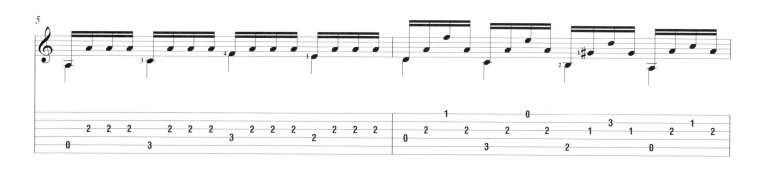

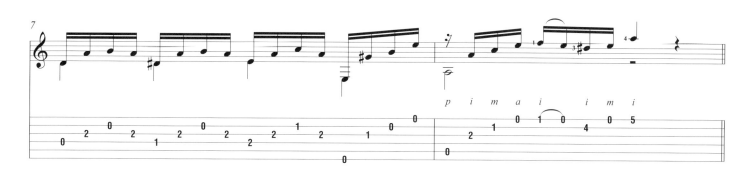

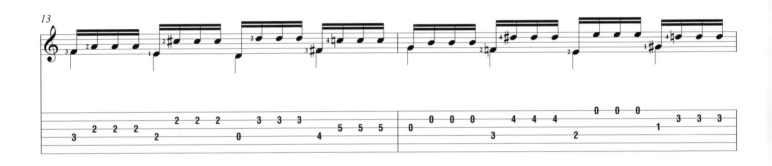

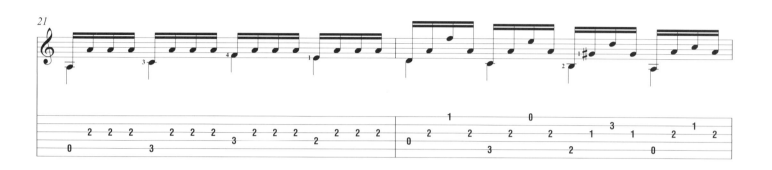

Repertoire

I've selected popular classical masterpieces, some of which are rarely heard on the guitar, and endeavoured to make arrangements that are idiomatic to the instrument and preserve as much of the original work as possible. The task of reducing a piano piece—or in some cases a symphony of instruments—to a solo guitar is challenging, but good music travels well and they have found a welcome home on the classical guitar.

Each piece is presented with musical notation, barré indications, fingerings, and guitar tablature. My performances of all of these arrangements are on the accompanying audio examples and I recommend listening to them, as well as listening to performances of the original works, so you can absorb such aspects of phrasing, flow, and dynamics that usually escape notation.

While many of these pieces are intermediate level—and I hope they bring you great pleasure to play—others are more difficult so be prepared to work with them for a while, breaking them into sections for practice sessions and taking long term goals. Regular, careful and patient work pays off, and is in fact the fastest way to success.

Enjoy your practice, and you'll be rewarded with wonderful pieces to perform for years to come.

Air on a G String

Johann Sebastian Bach
Arranged by Bridget Mermikides

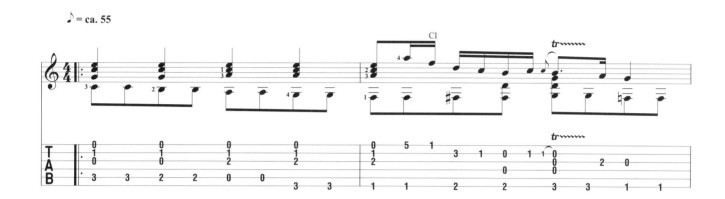

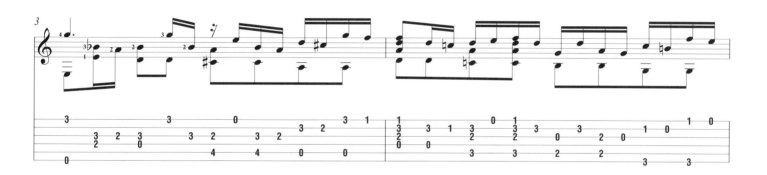

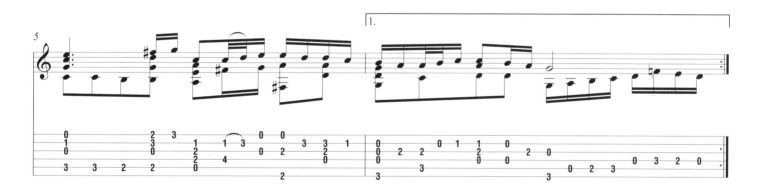

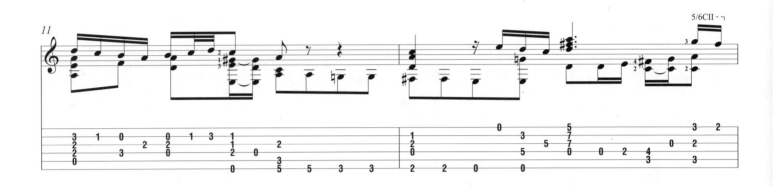

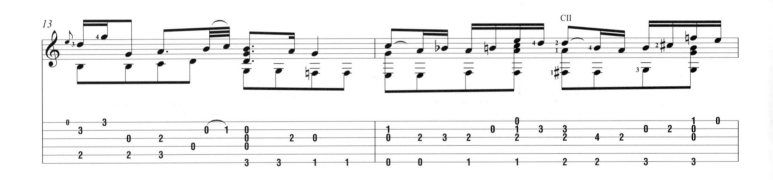

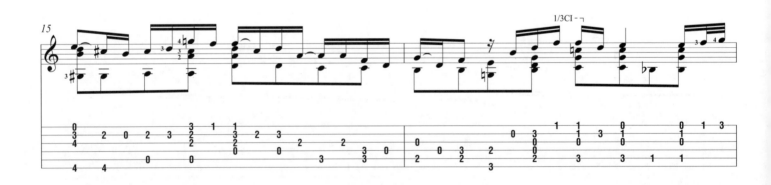

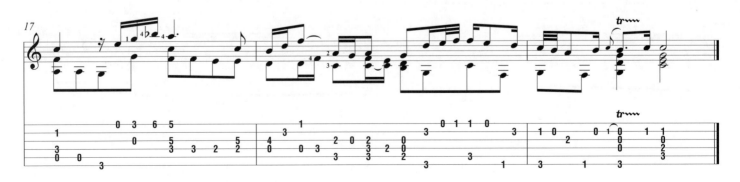

Jesu Joy of Man's Desiring

Johann Sebastian Bach
Arranged by Bridget Mermikides

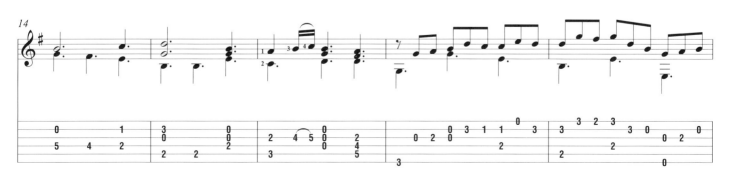

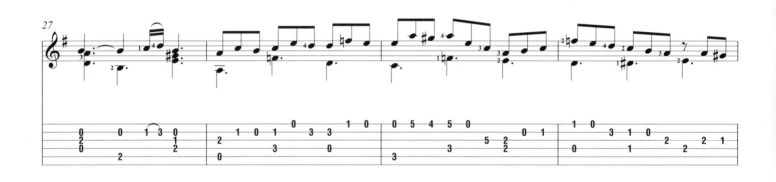

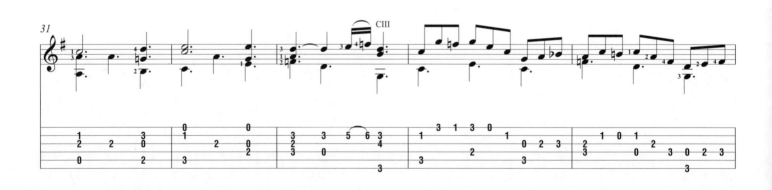

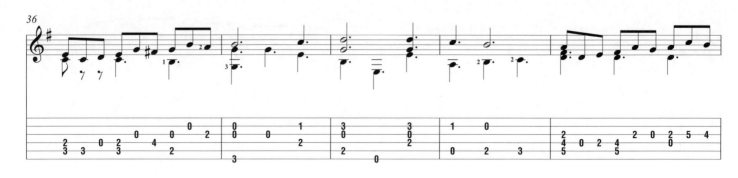

Prelude from Cello Suite No. 1

Johann Sebastian Bach
Arranged by Bridget Mermikides

Drop D tuning:
(low to high) D-A-D-G-B-E

♩ = ca. 64

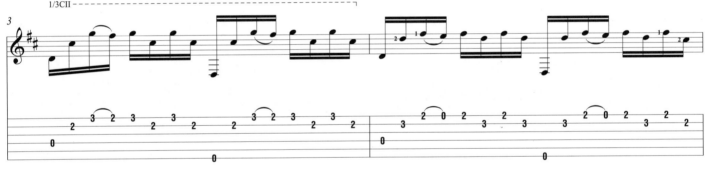

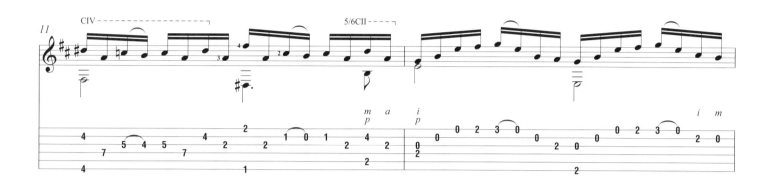

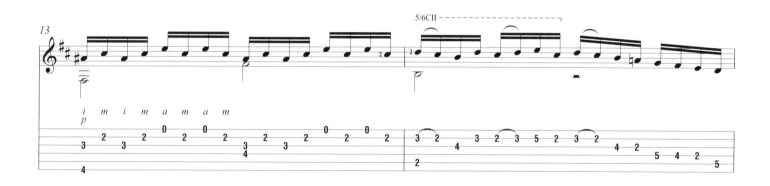

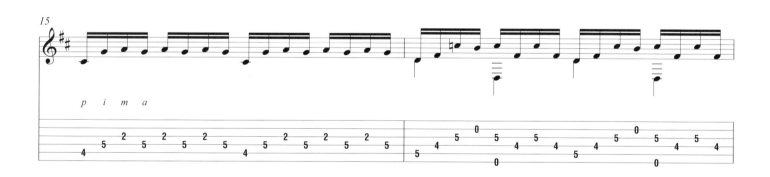

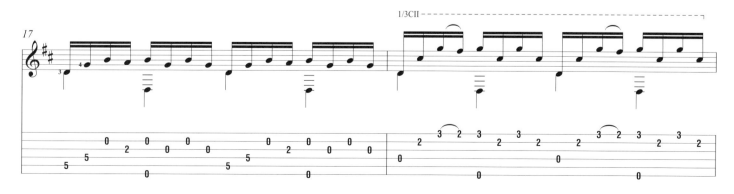

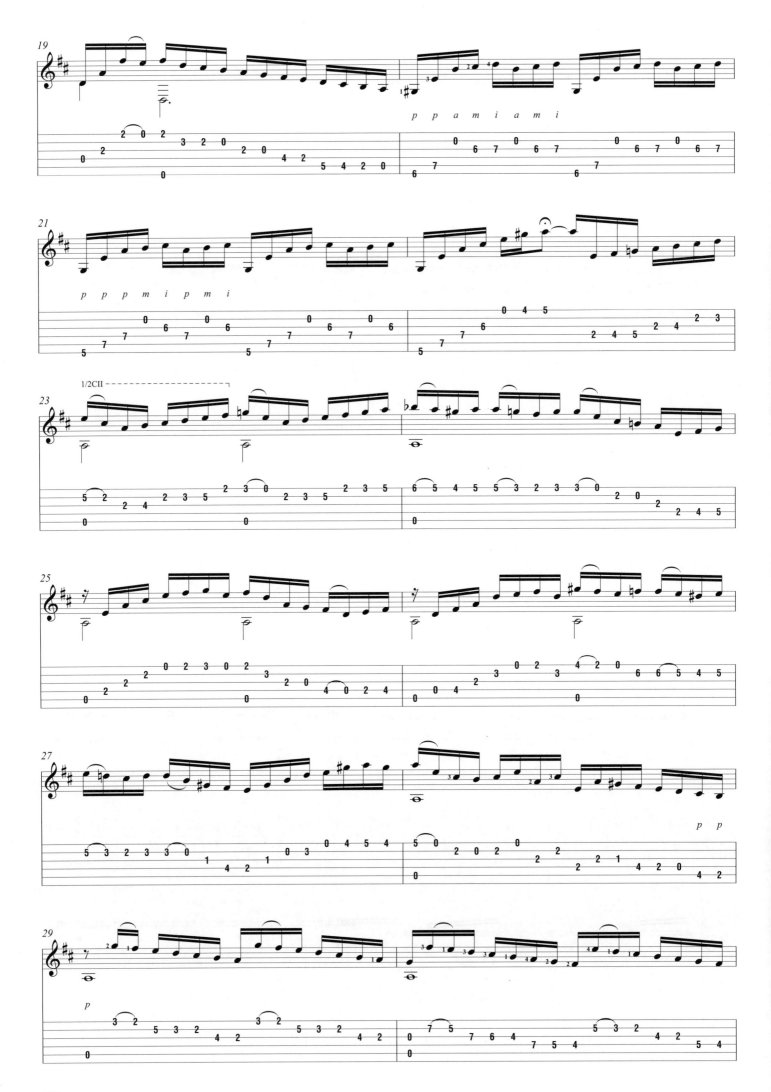

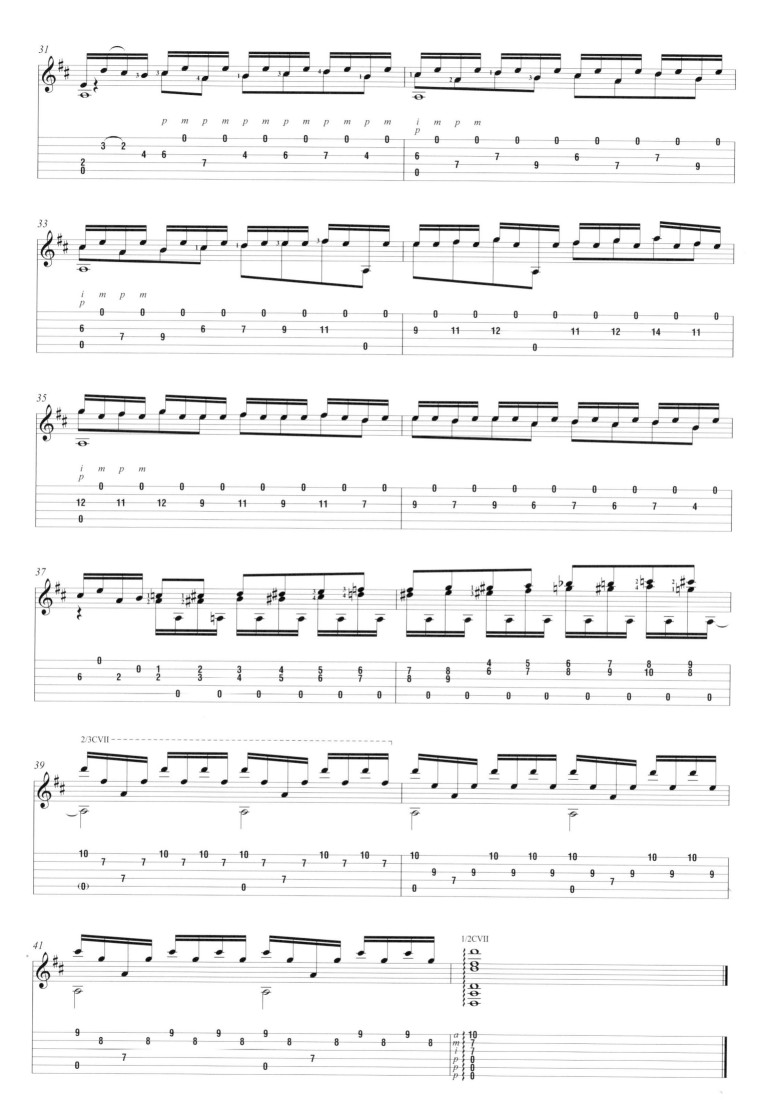

Adagio from Pathetique Sonata

Ludwig van Beethoven
Arranged by Bridget Mermikides

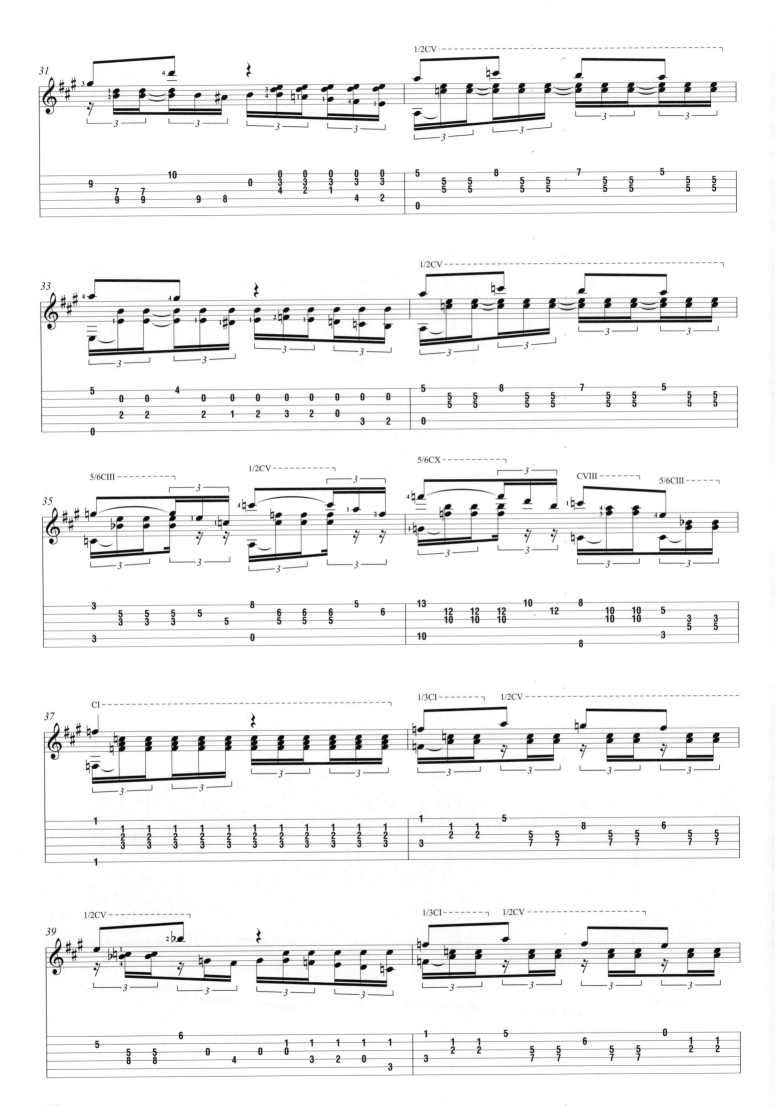

let ring throughout

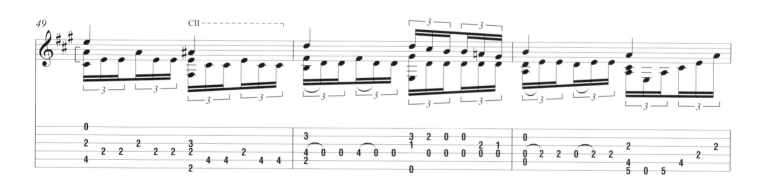

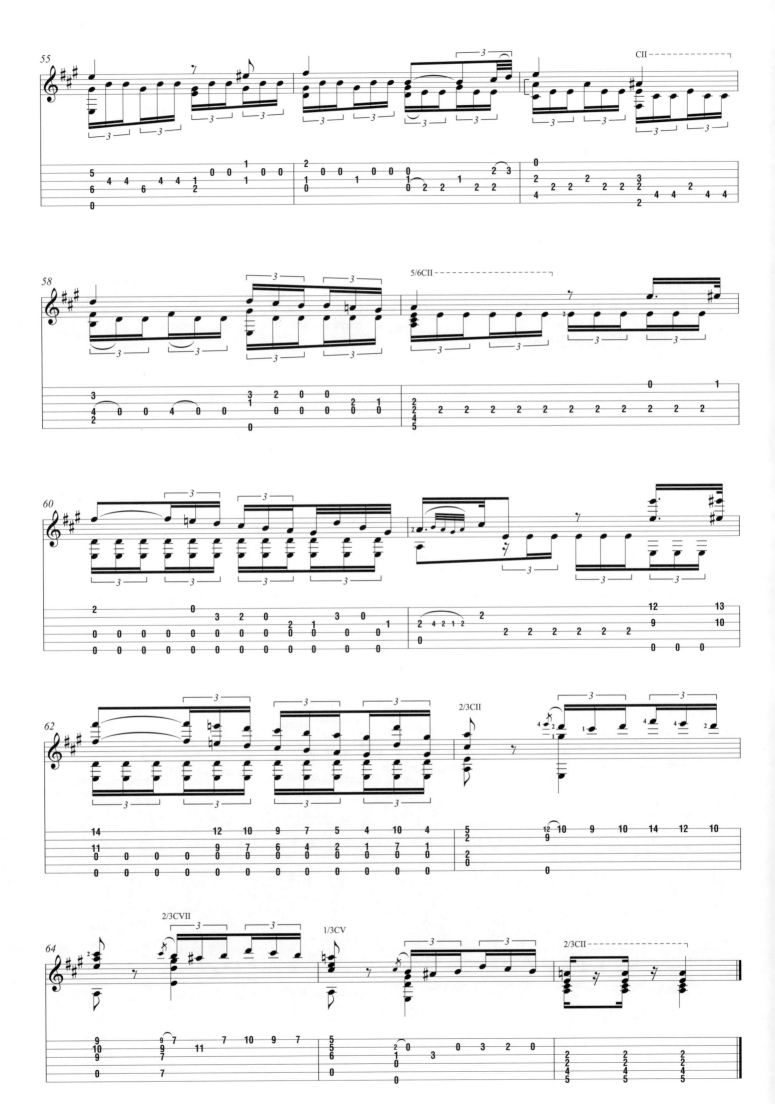

Für Elise

Ludwig van Beethoven
Arranged by Bridget Mermikides

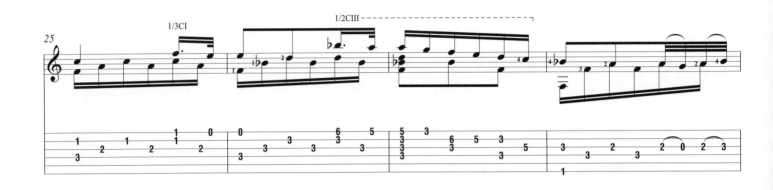

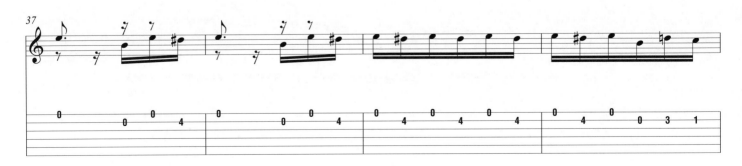

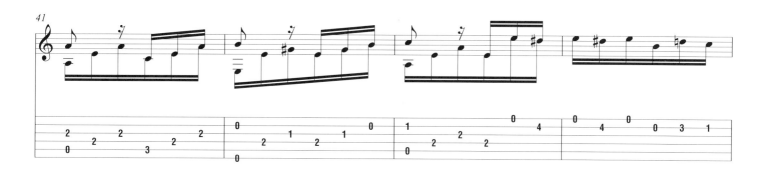

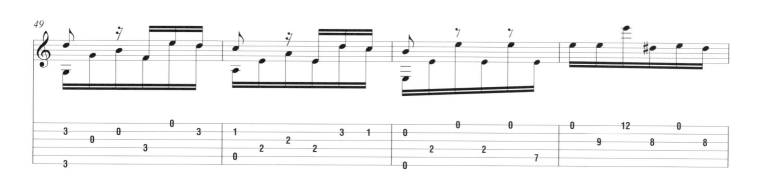

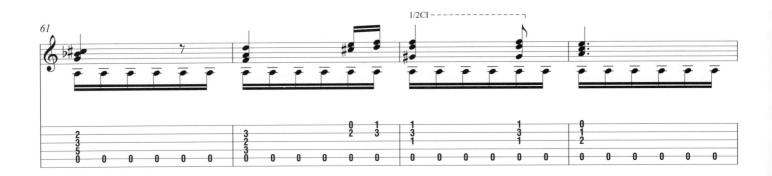

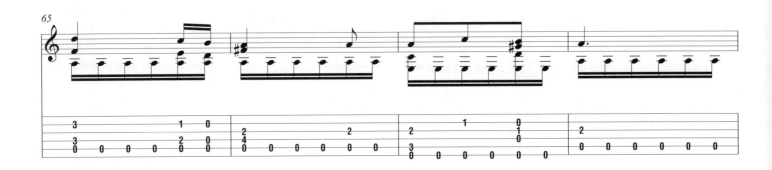

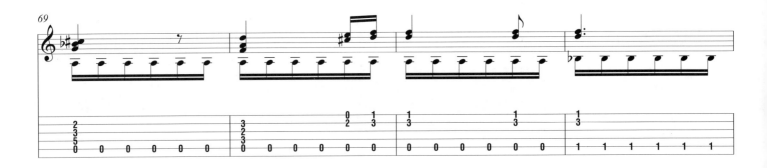

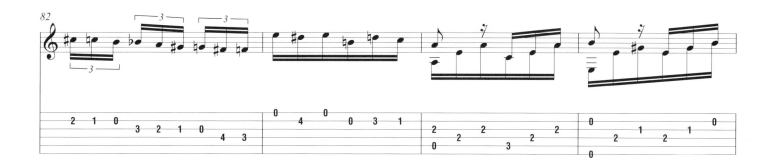

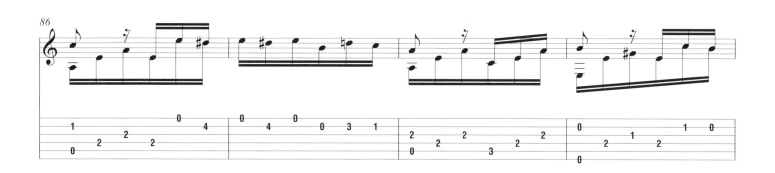

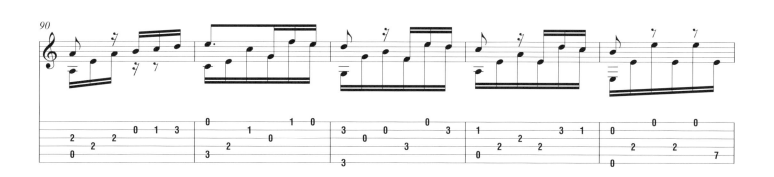

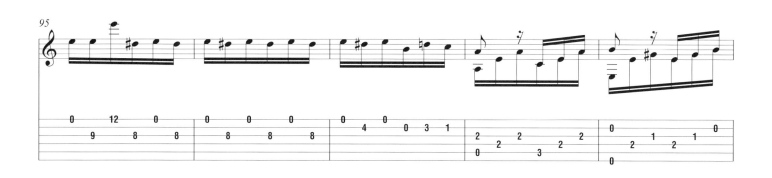

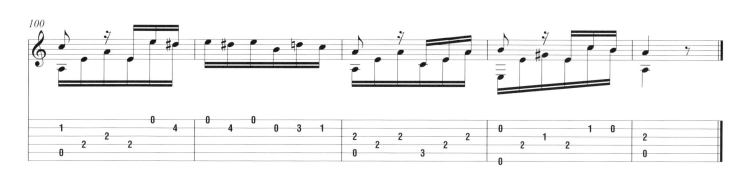

Moonlight Sonata

Ludwig van Beethoven
Arranged by Bridget Mermikides

Adagio sostenuto

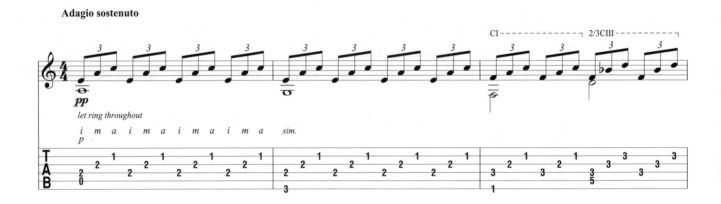

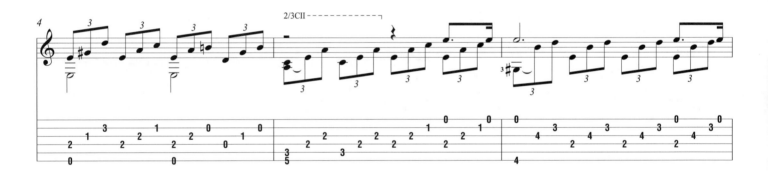

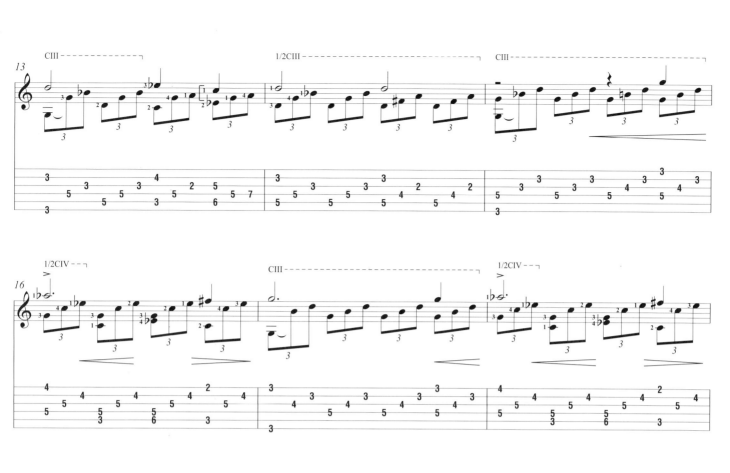

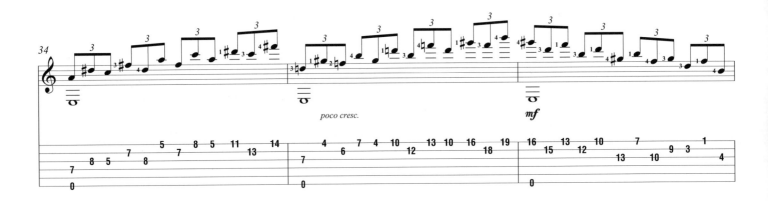

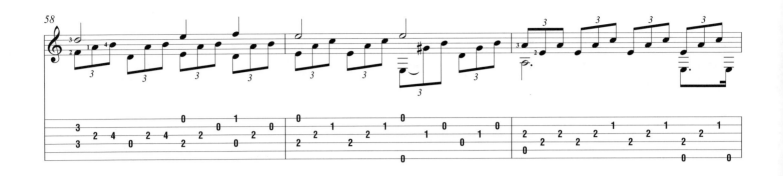

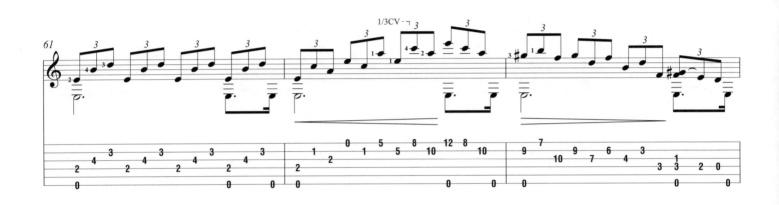

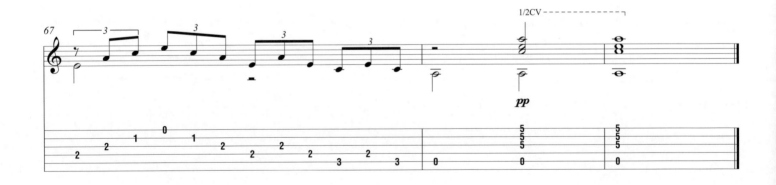

Lullaby

Johannes Brahms
Arranged by Bridget Mermikides

*Capo I, Drop D tuning:
(low to high) D-A-D-G-B-E

Delicatamente molto

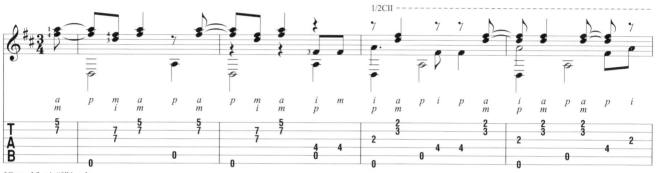

*Capoed fret is "0" in tab.

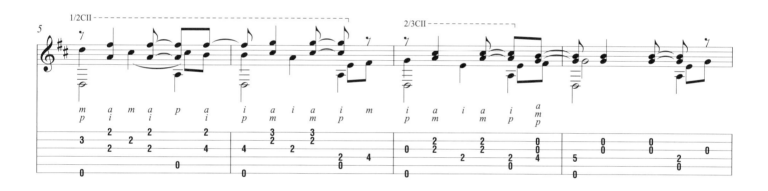

Nocturne Opus 9 No. 2

Frédéric Chopin
Arranged by Bridget Mermikides

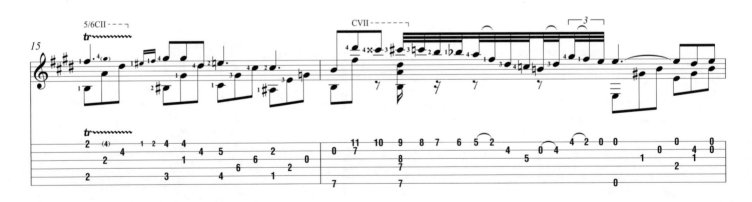

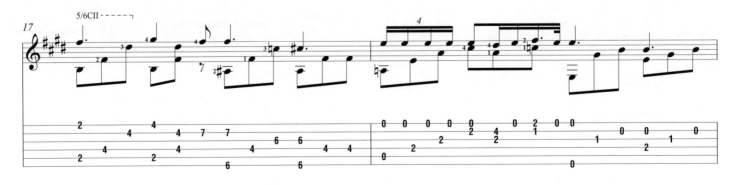

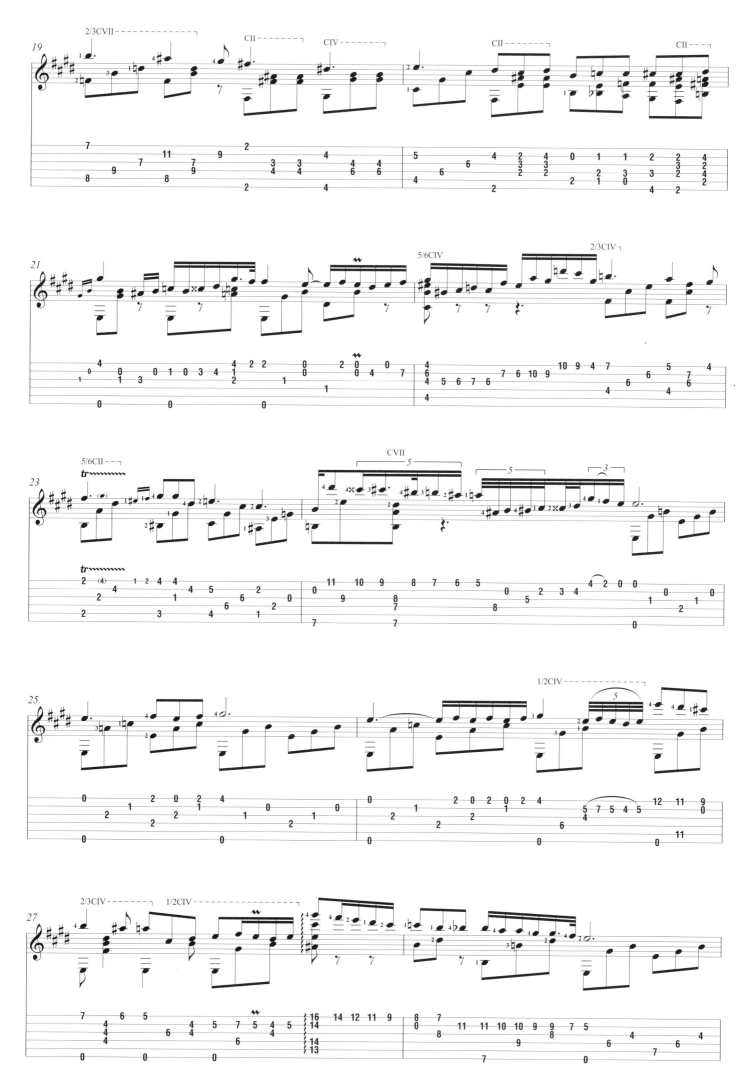

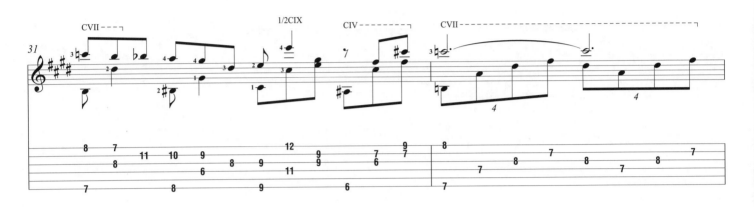

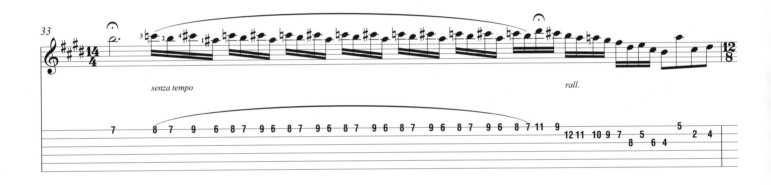

Prelude Opus 28 No. 4

Frédéric Chopin
Arranged by Bridget Mermikides

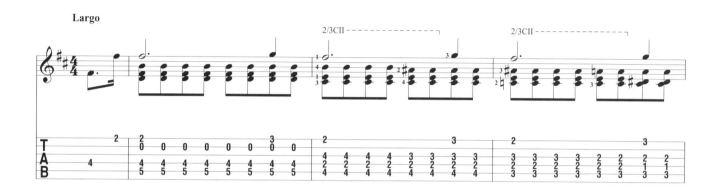

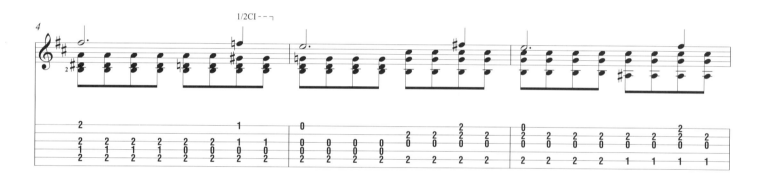

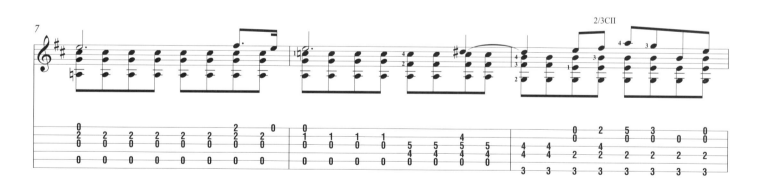

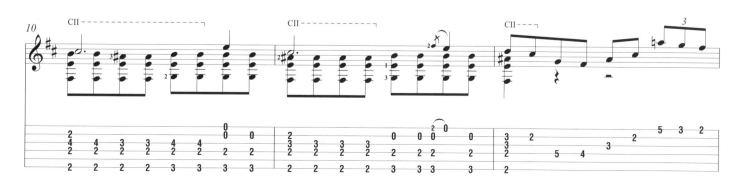

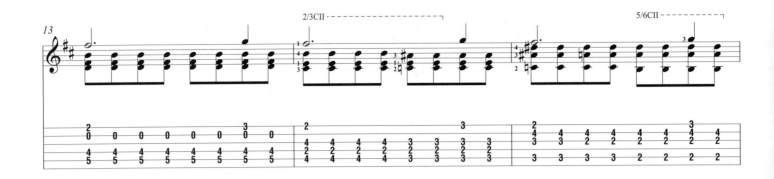

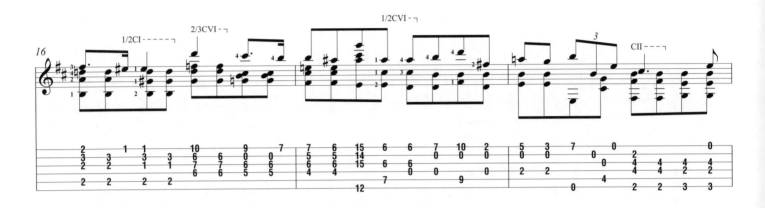

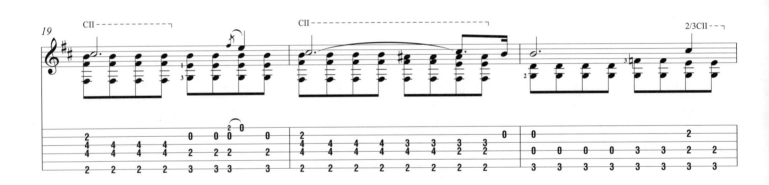

Prelude Opus 28 No. 20

Frédéric Chopin
Arranged by Bridget Mermikides

Clair de Lune

Claude Debussy
Arranged by Bridget Mermikides

Andante très expressif

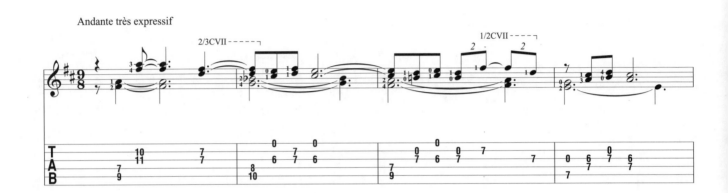

*Use hinge barre.

*Hold down bass note using hinge barre.

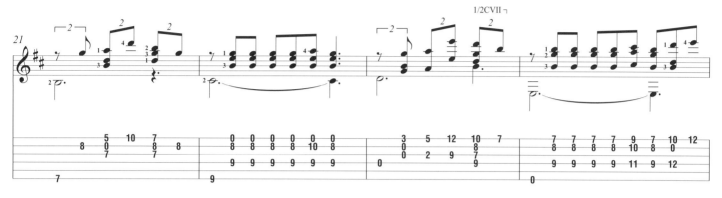

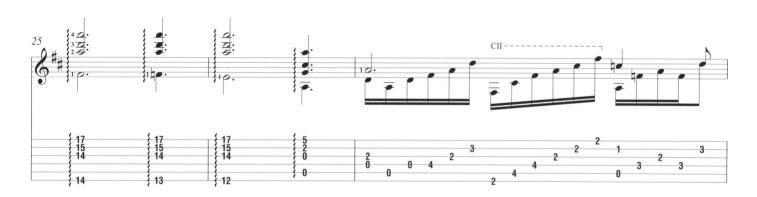

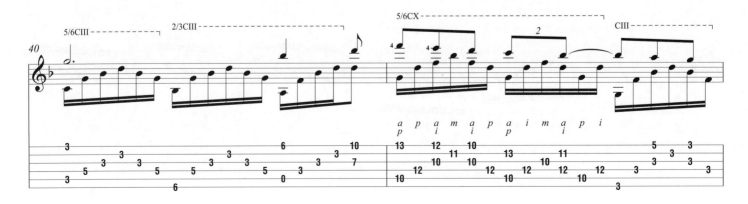

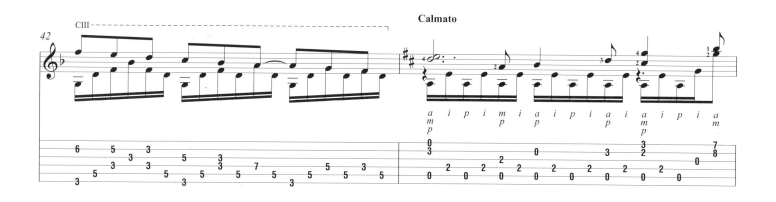

Calmato

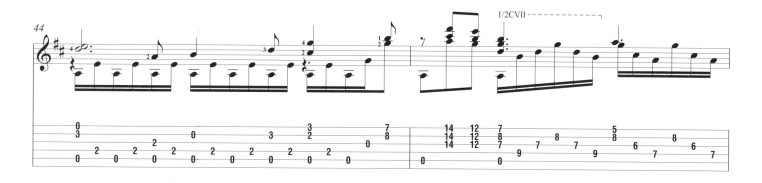

*Harm.

*Harm. refers to upstem note only.

Tempo I

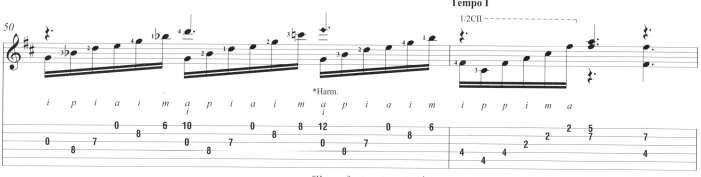

*Harm.

*Harm. refers to upstem note only.

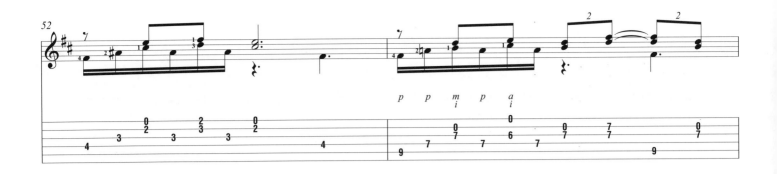

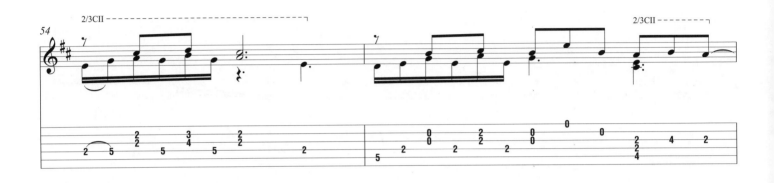

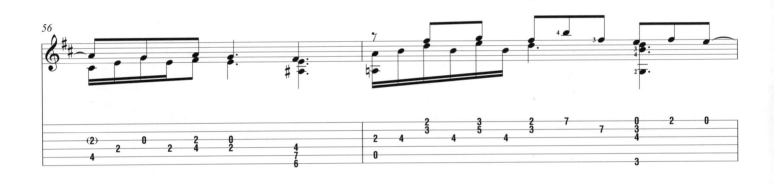

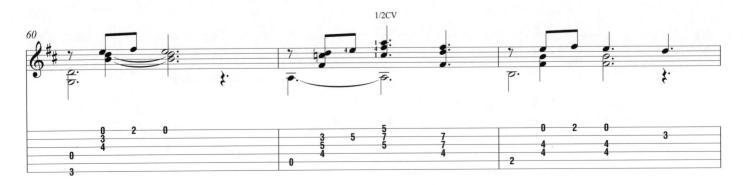

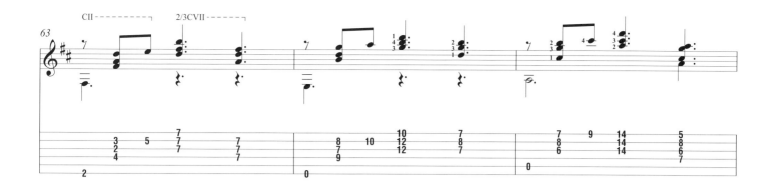

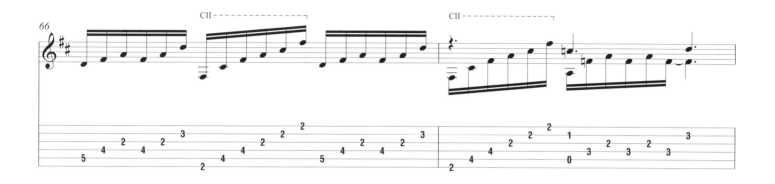

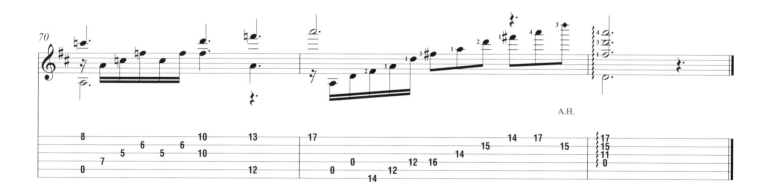

La Fille aux Cheveux de Lin

Claude Debussy
Arranged by Bridget Mermikides

Tres calme et doucement expressif

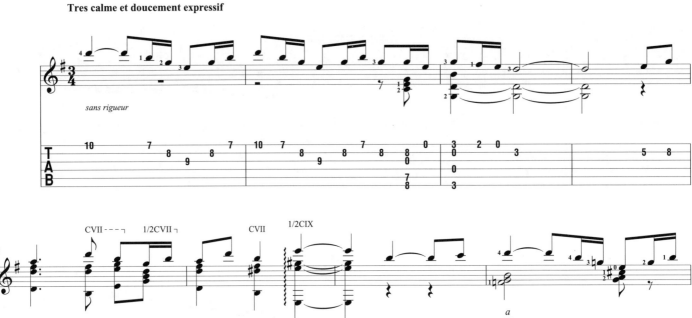

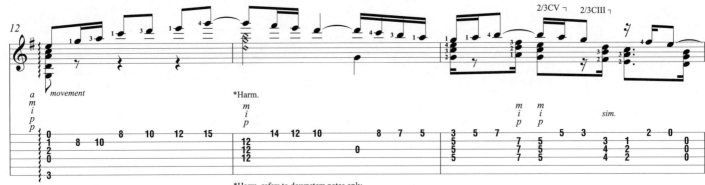

*Harm. refers to downstem notes only.

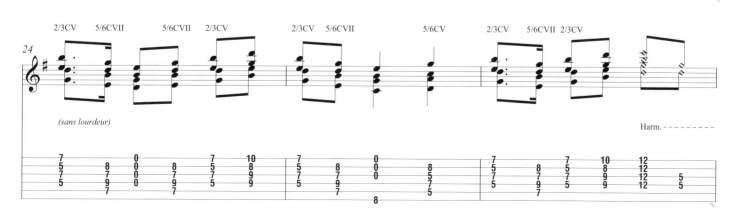

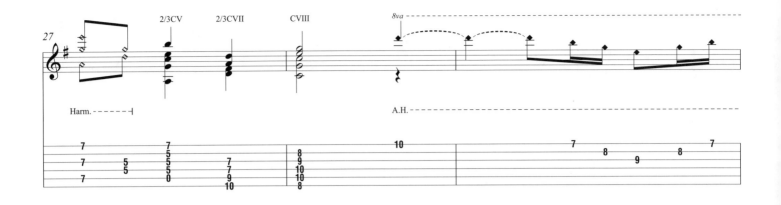

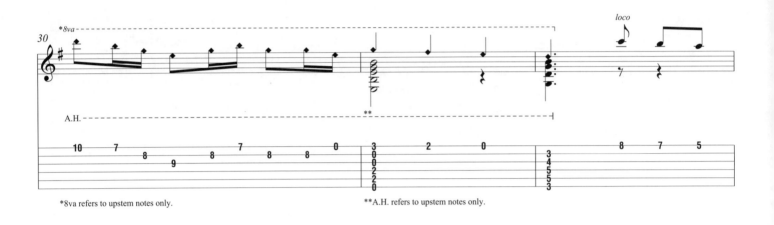

*8va refers to upstem notes only.

**A.H. refers to upstem notes only.

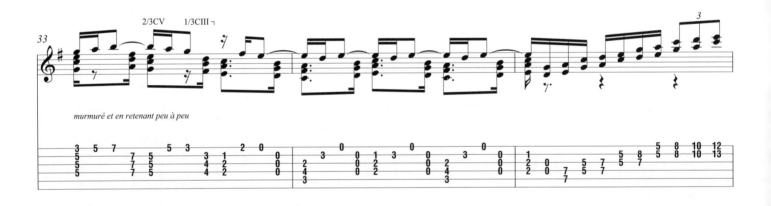

murmuré et en retenant peu à peu

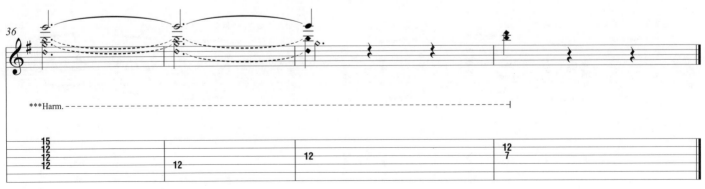

***Harm. refers to downstem notes only.

Flower Duet from Lakmé

Léo Delibes
Arranged by Bridget Mermikides

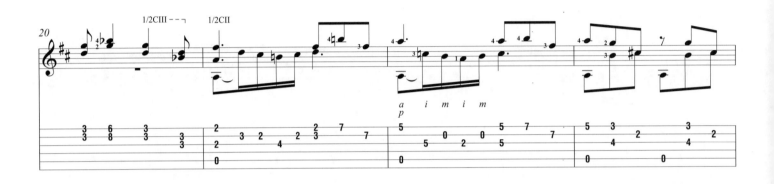

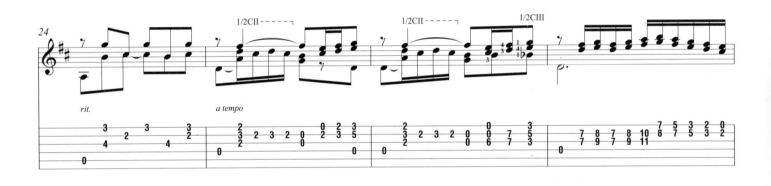

Pavane

Gabriel Fauré
Arranged by Bridget Mermikides

Andante molto moderato

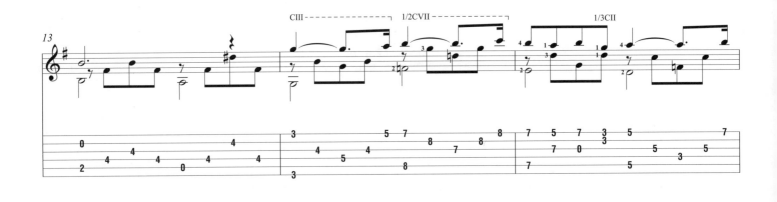

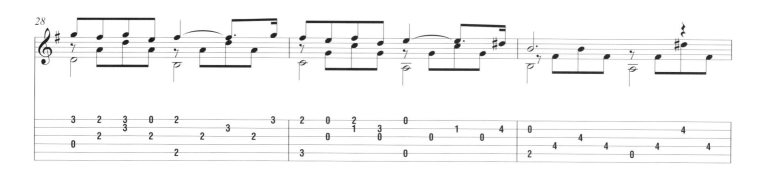

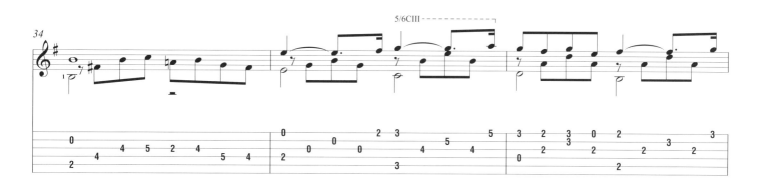

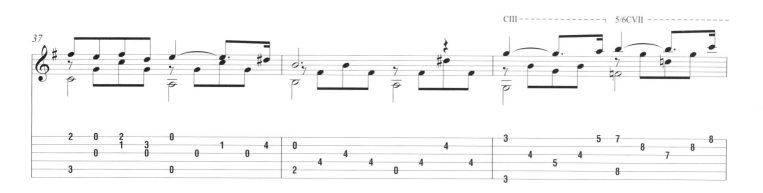

Hall of the Mountain King

Edvard Grieg
Arranged by Bridget Mermikides

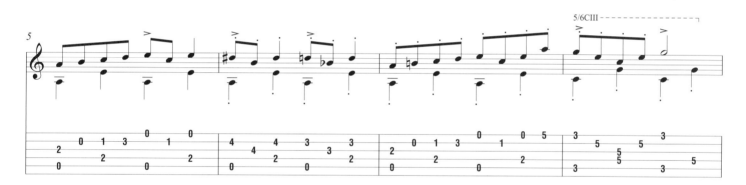

*Use hinge barre for open 6th string.

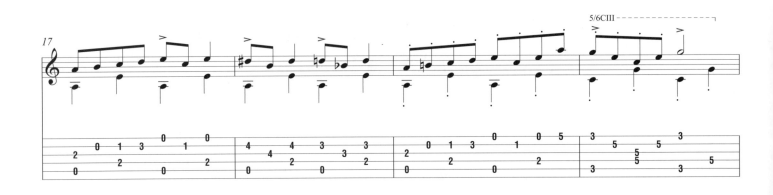

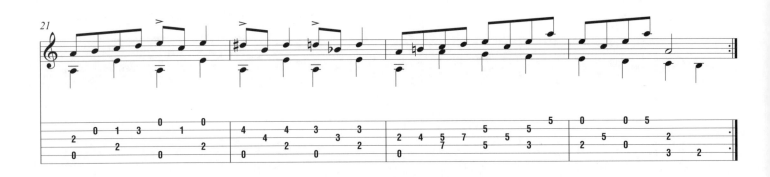

più vivo

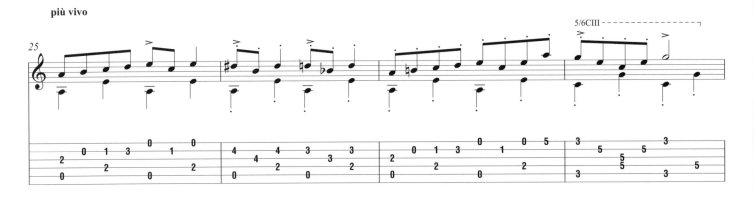

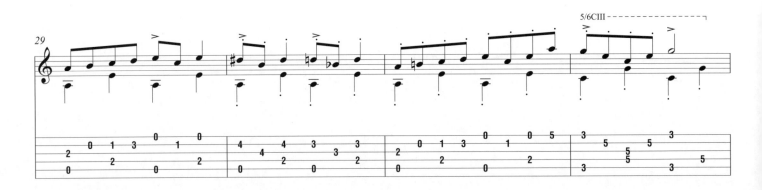

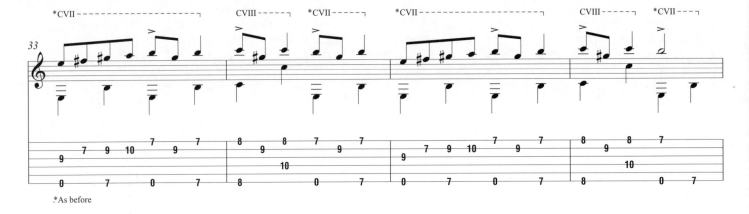

*As before

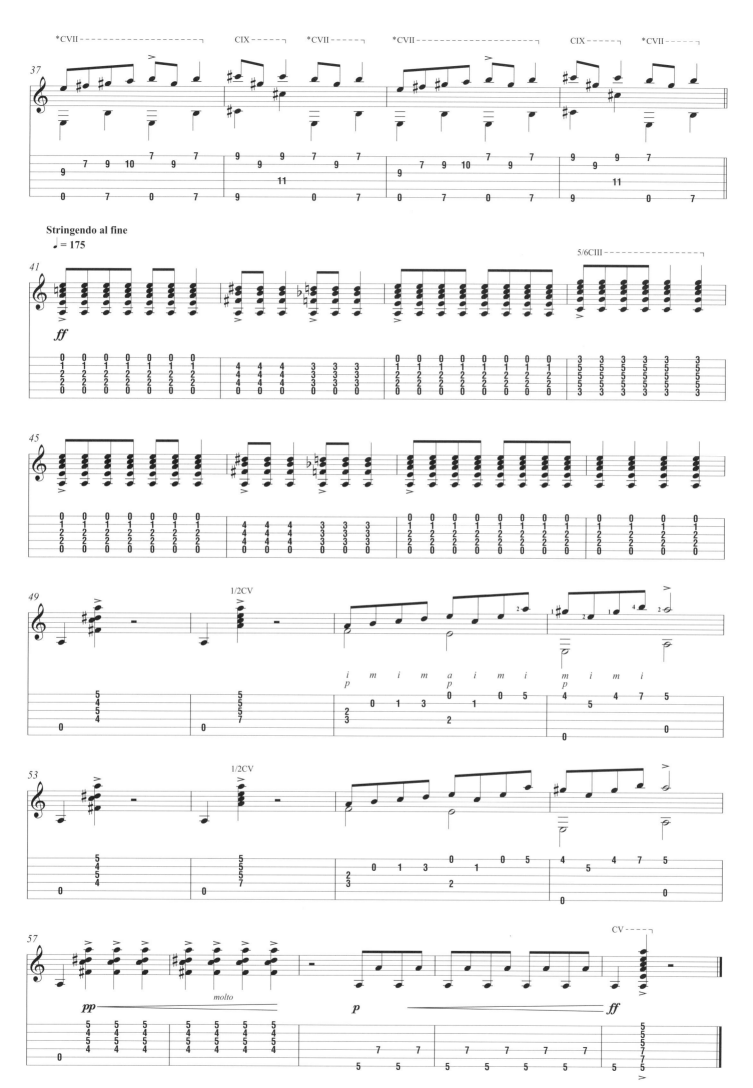

Morning Mood from Peer Gynt

Edvard Grieg
Arranged by Bridget Mermikides

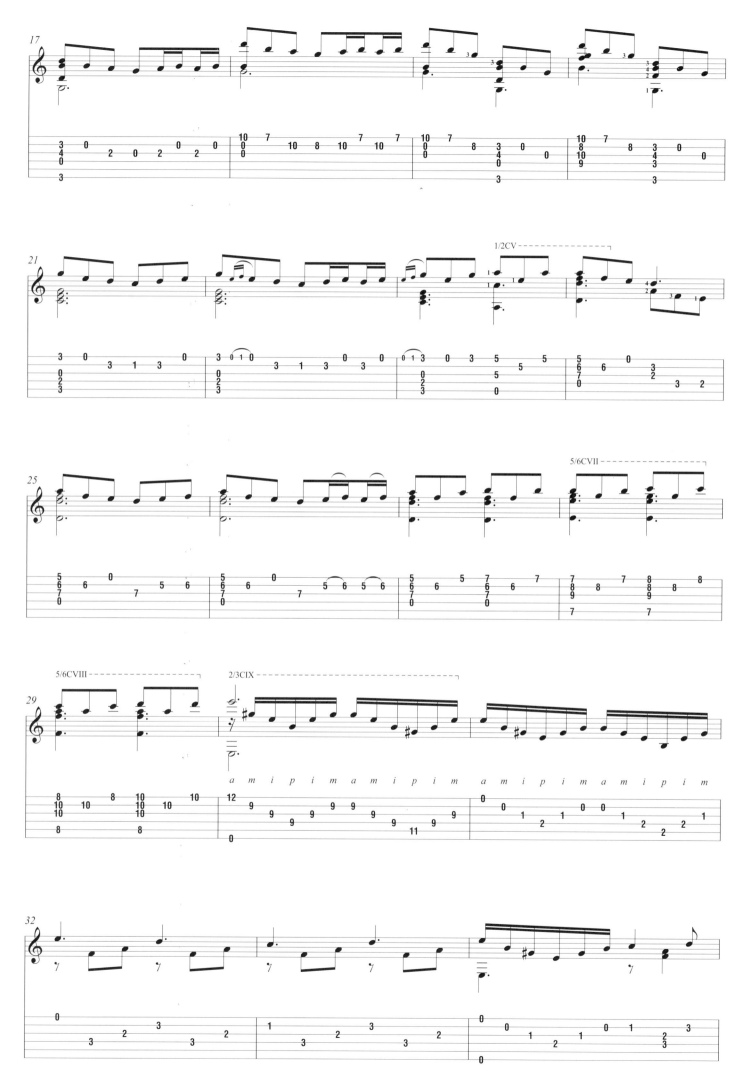

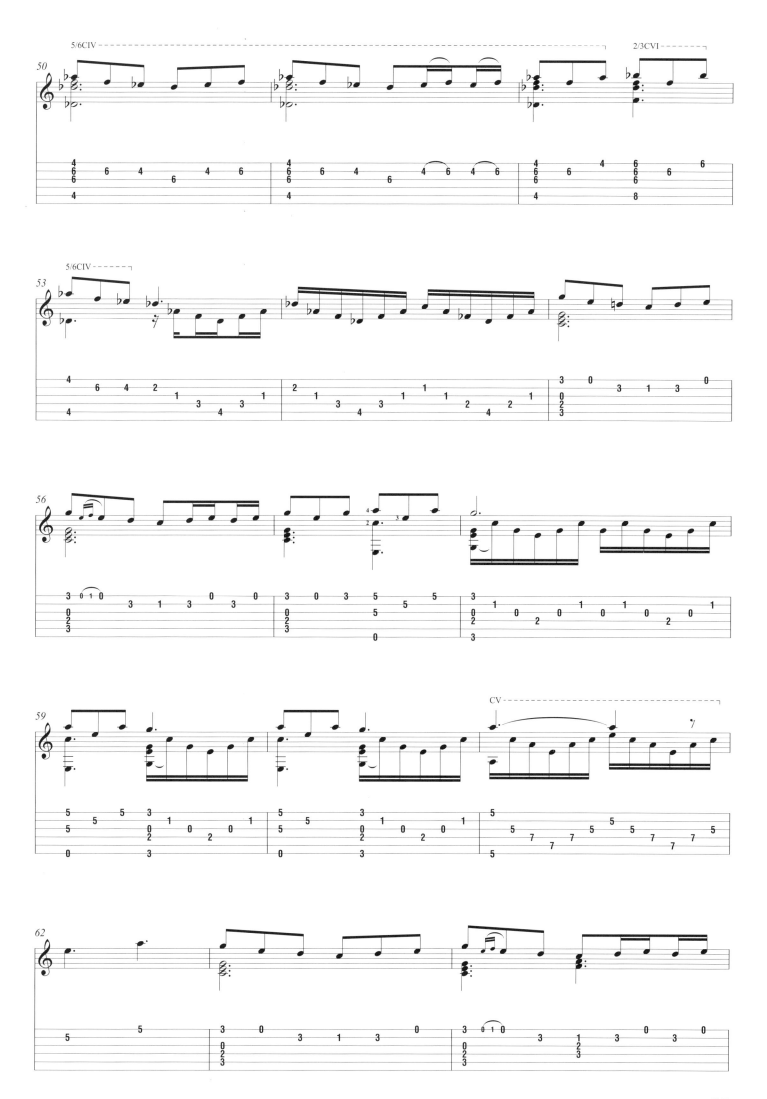

Méditation from Thaïs

Jules Massenet
Arranged by Bridget Mermikides

Drop D tuning:
(low to high) D-A-D-G-B-E

Andante

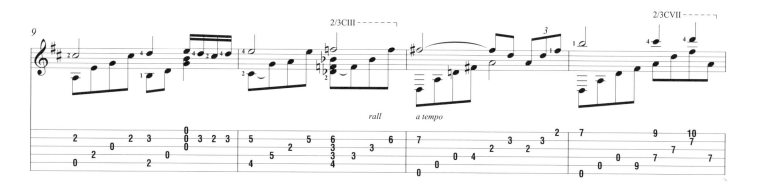

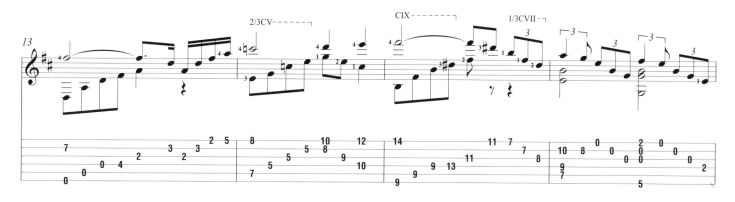

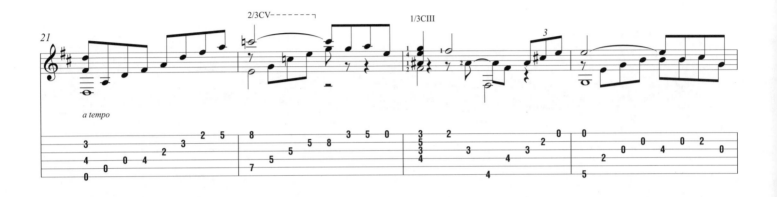

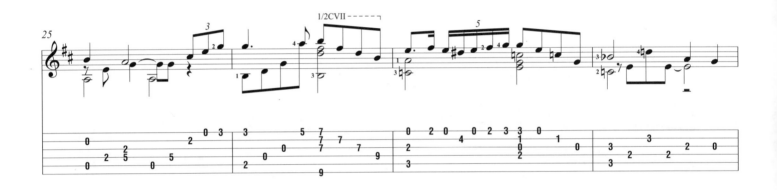

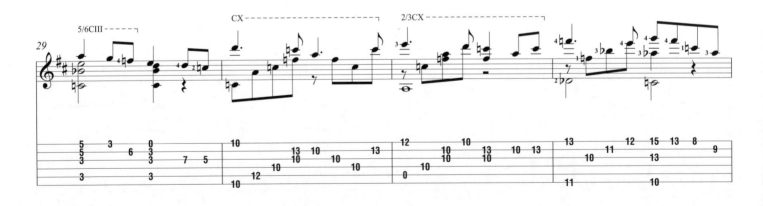

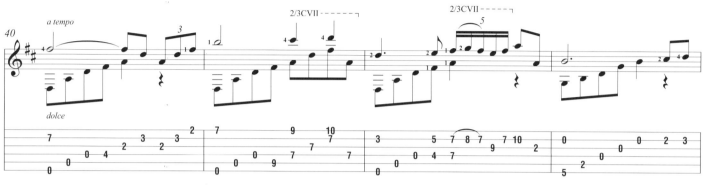

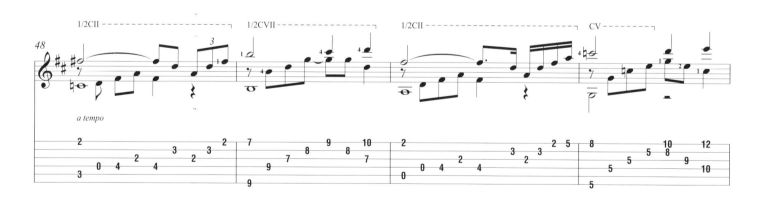

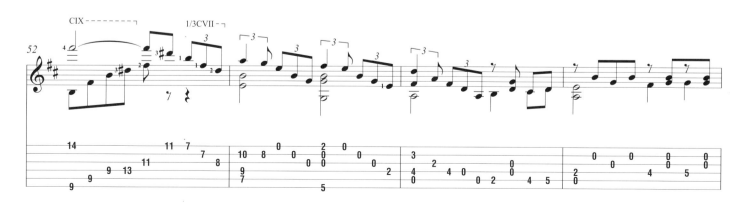

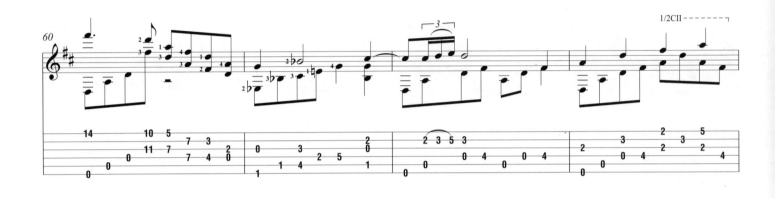

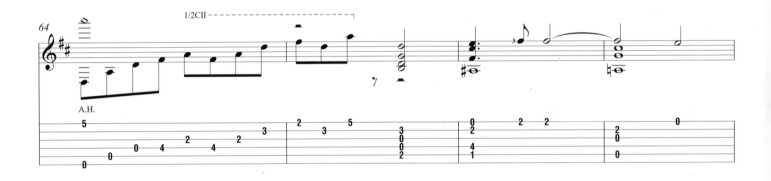

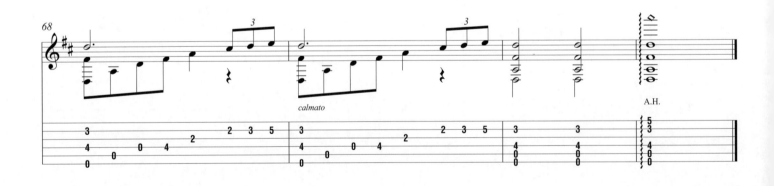

Clarinet Concerto 2nd Movement

Wolfgang Amadeus Mozart
Arranged by Bridget Mermikides

Drop D tuning:
(low to high) D-A-D-G-B-E

Adagio

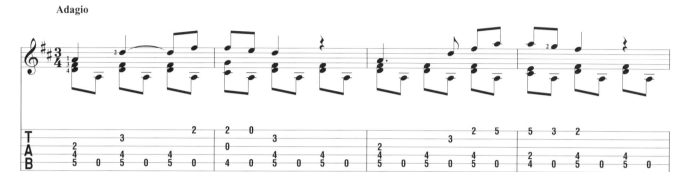

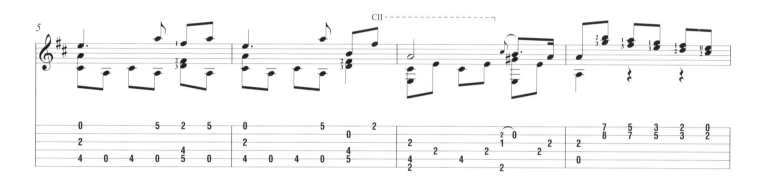

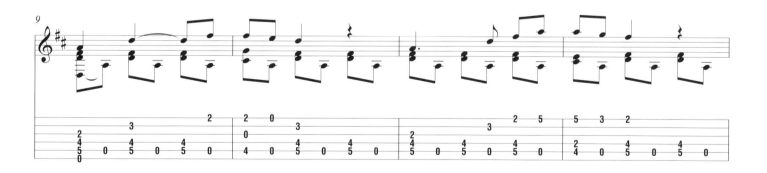

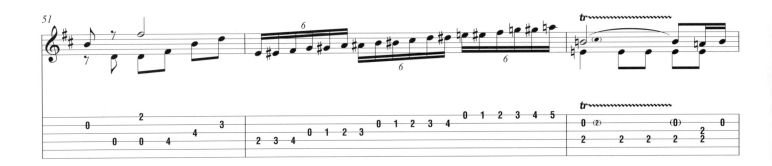

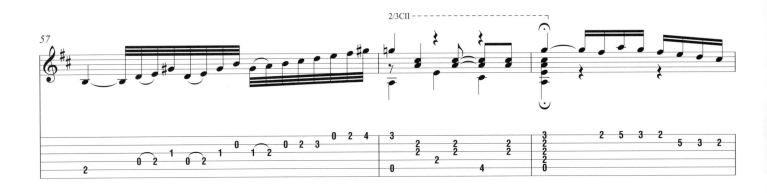

Piano Concerto No. 21 Andante

Wolfgang Amadeus Mozart
Arranged by Bridget Mermikides

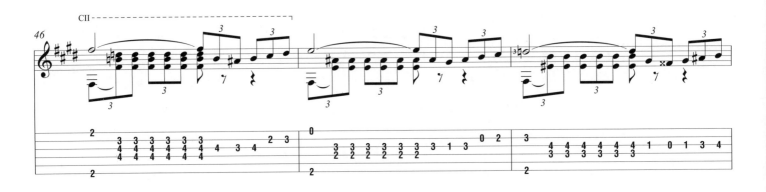

Rondo alla Turca

Wolfgang Amadeus Mozart
Arranged by Bridget Mermikides

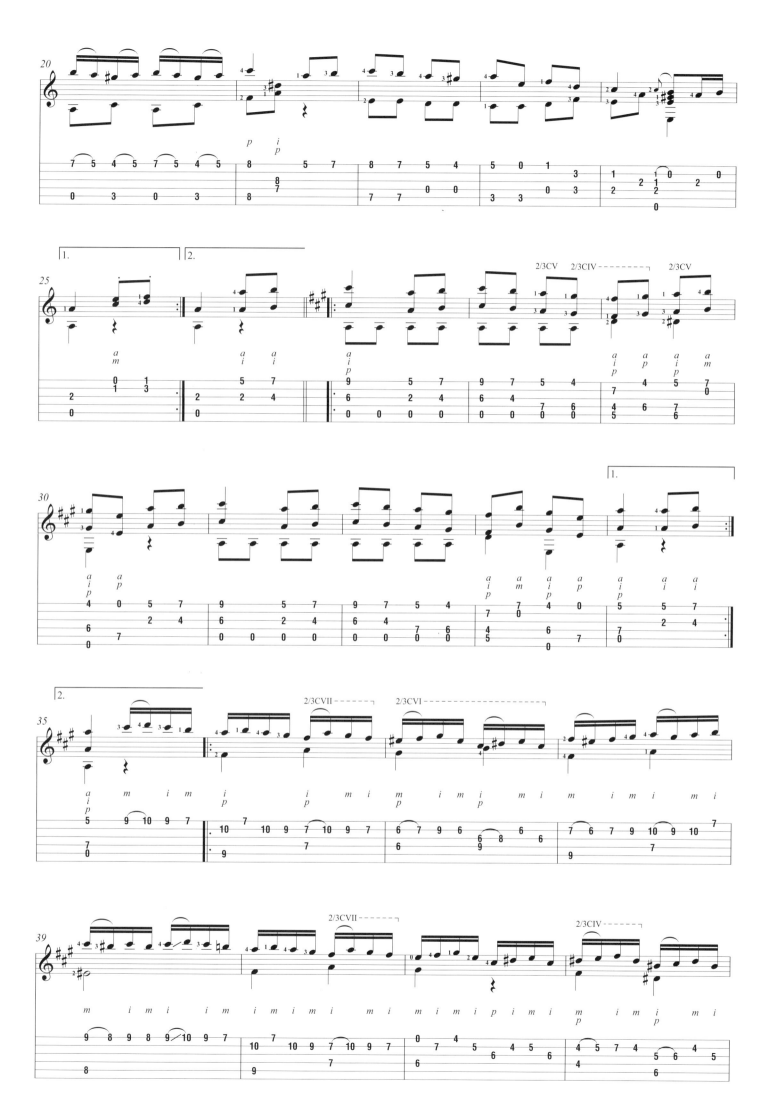

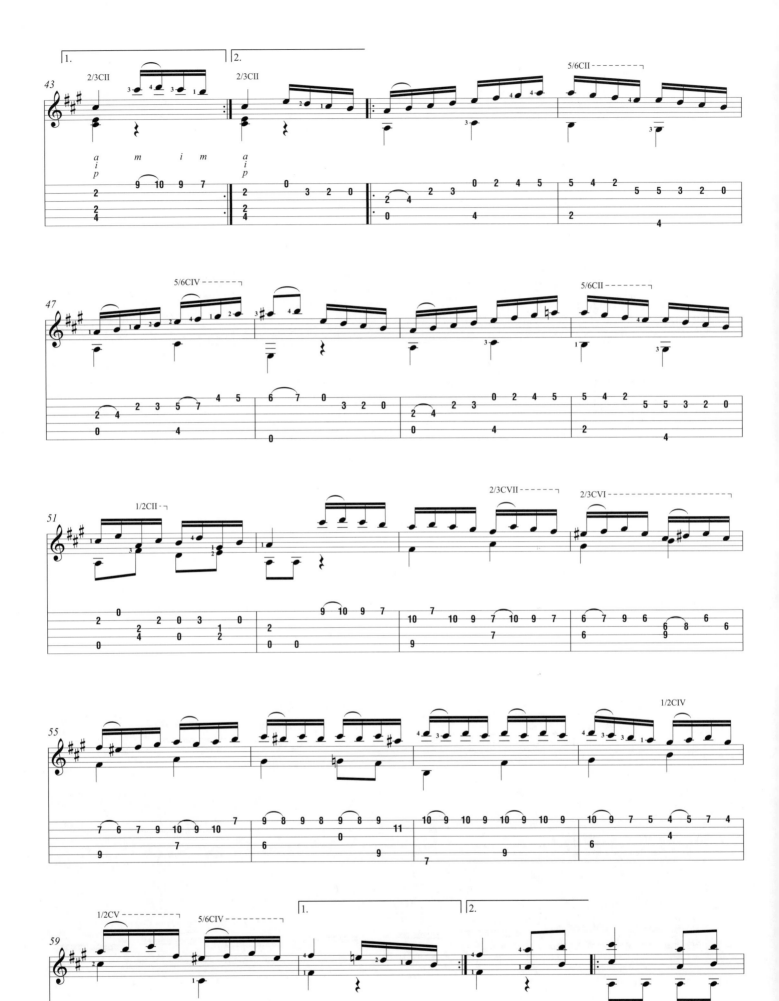

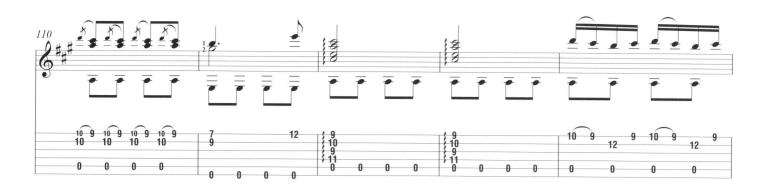

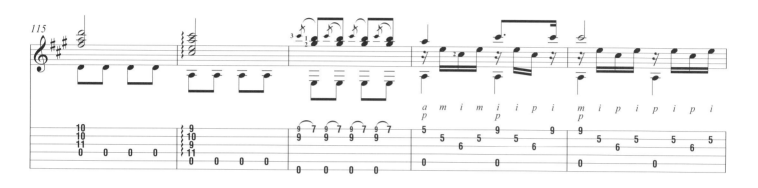

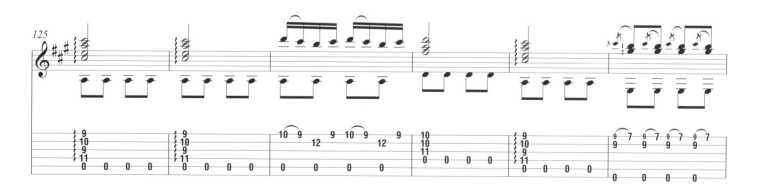

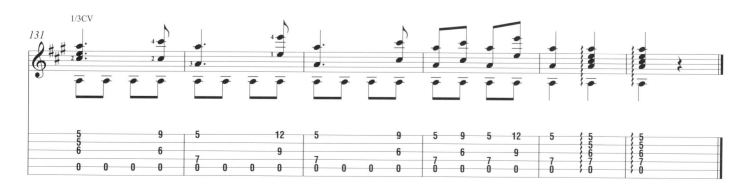

Canon

Johann Pachelbel
Arranged by Bridget Mermikides

Drop D tuning:
(low to high) D-A-D-G-B-E

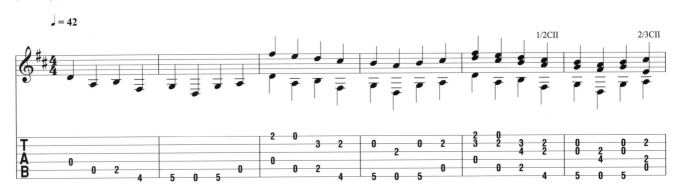

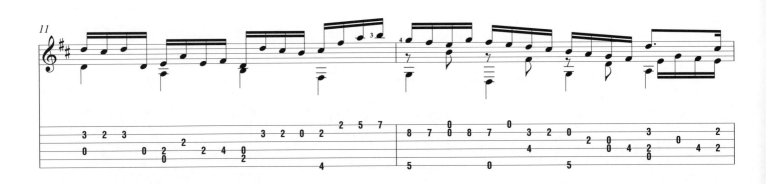

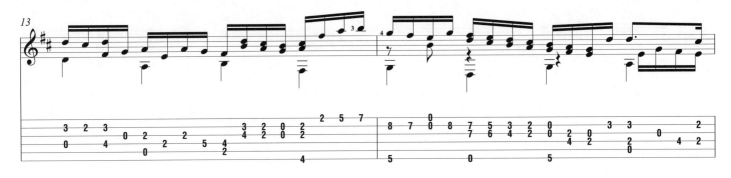

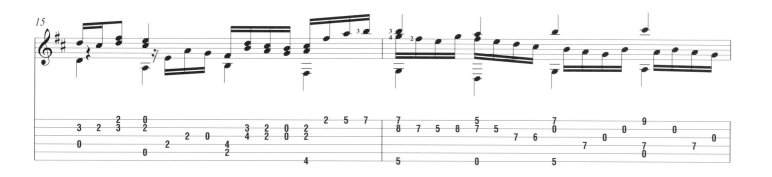

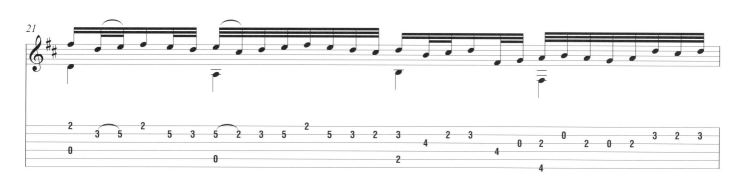

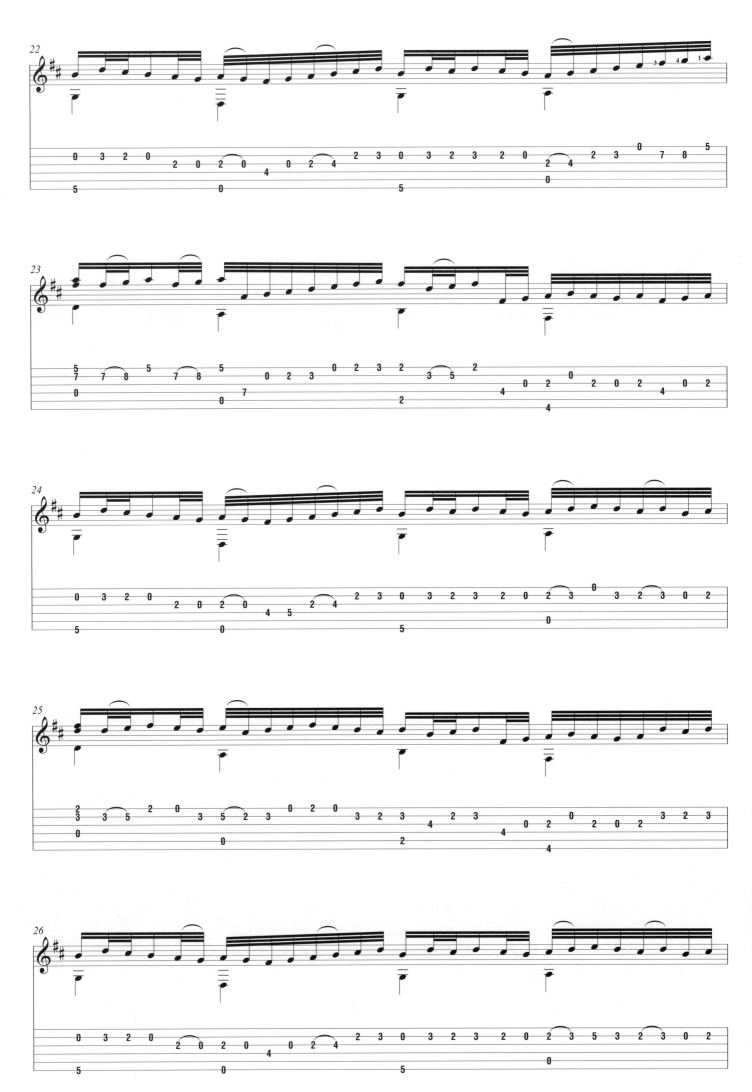

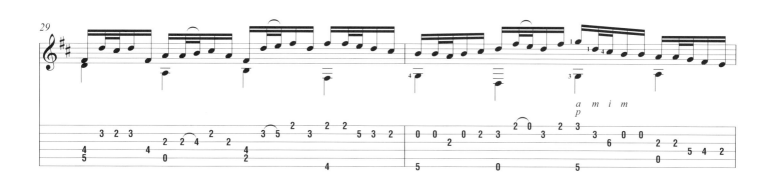

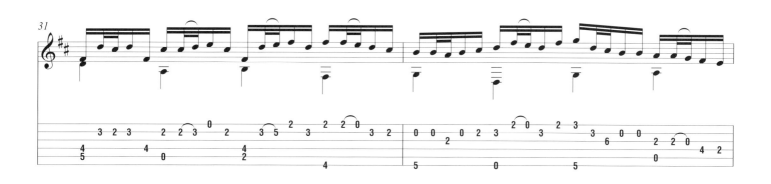

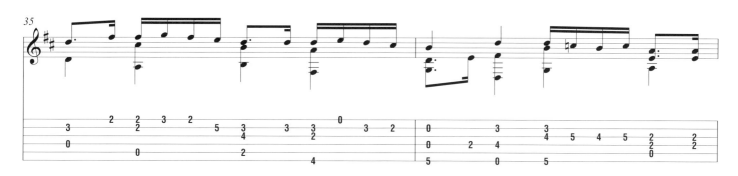

Nessun Dorma

Giacomo Puccini
Arranged by Bridget Mermikides

Tuning:
(low to high) D-G-D-G-B-E

Expressively with rubato

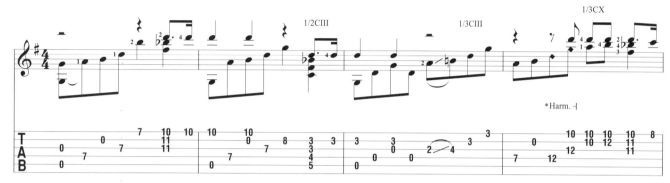

*Harm. refers to downstem notes only.

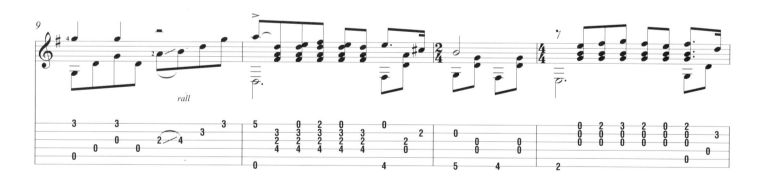

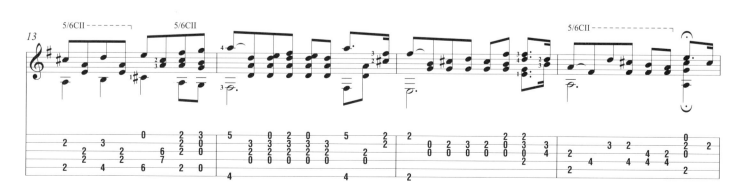

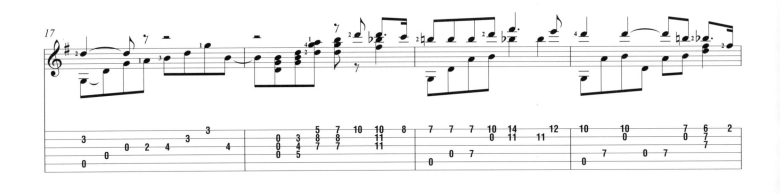

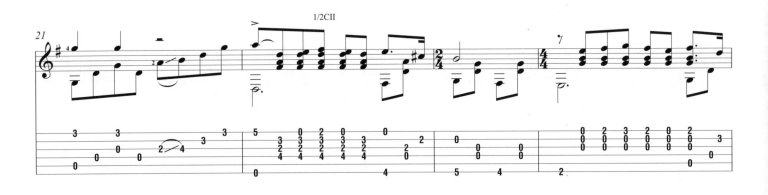

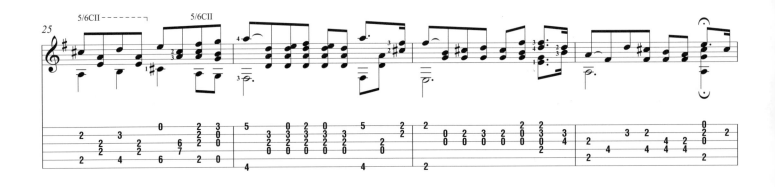

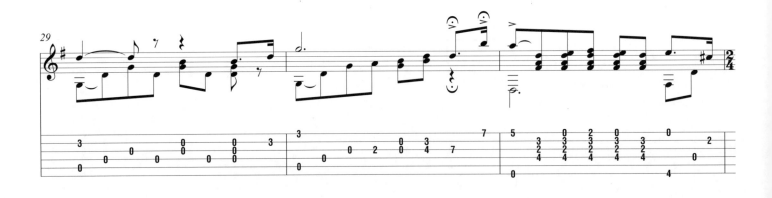

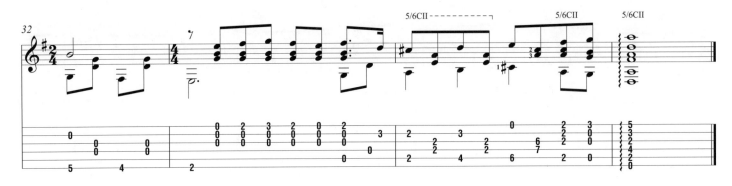

Bolero

Maurice Ravel
Arranged by Bridget Mermikides

Tuning:
(low to high) C-G-C-G-B-E

Moderato assai

*Palm mute bass line, but not melody.

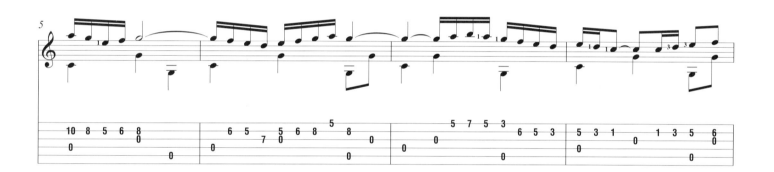

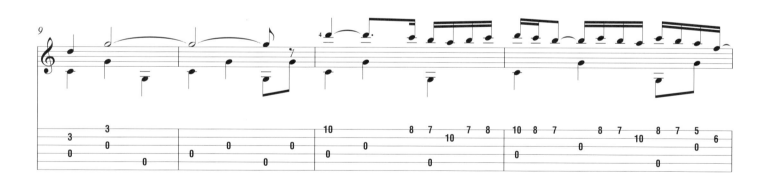

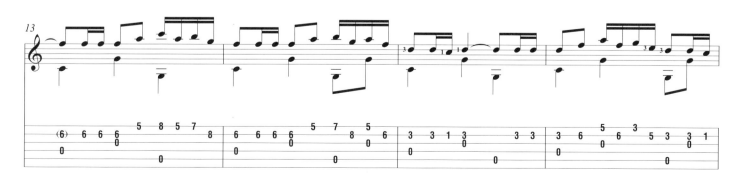

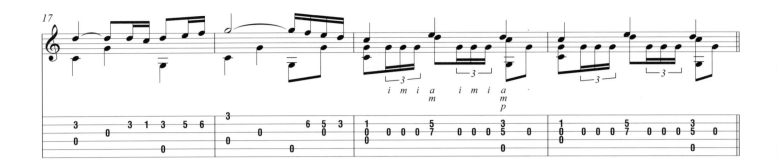

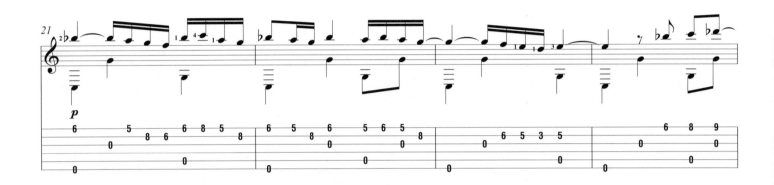

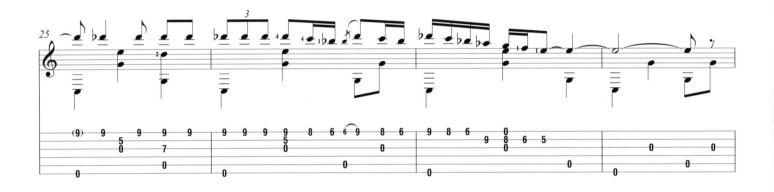

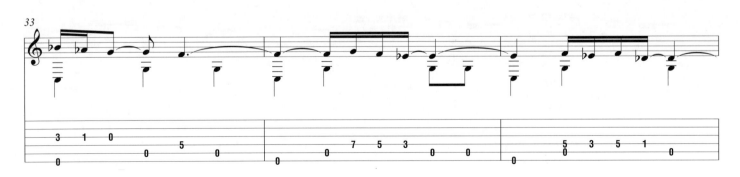

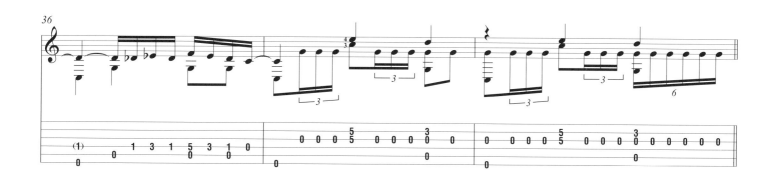

*Continue palm muting bass line where possible.

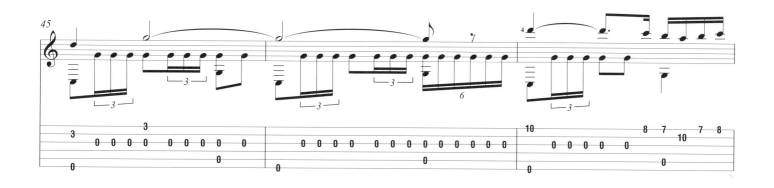

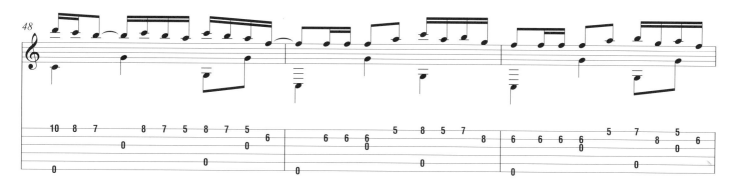

*Use hinge barre for open strings.

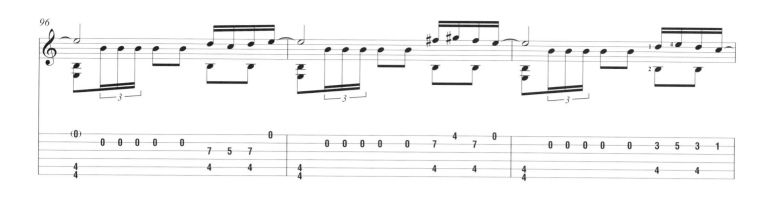

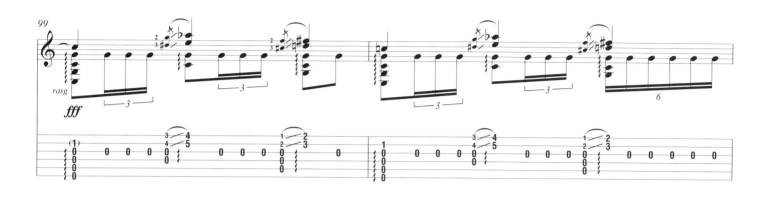

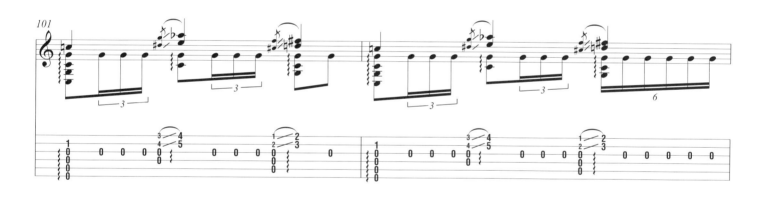

Gnossienne No. 1

Erik Satie
Arranged by Bridget Mermikides

Du bout de la pensée

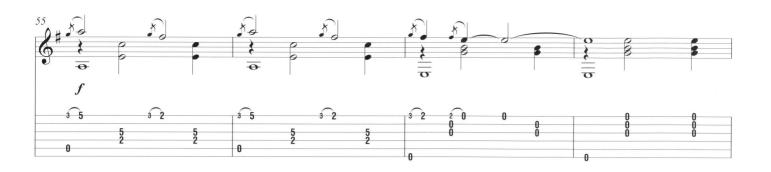

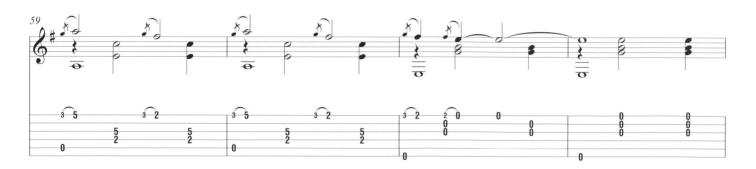

Postulez en vous-même

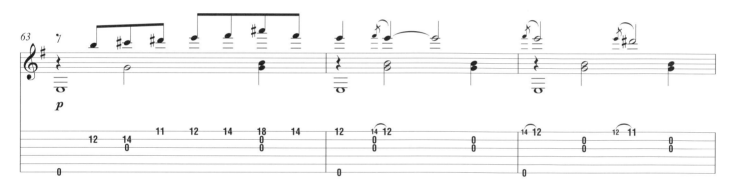

Pas à Pas

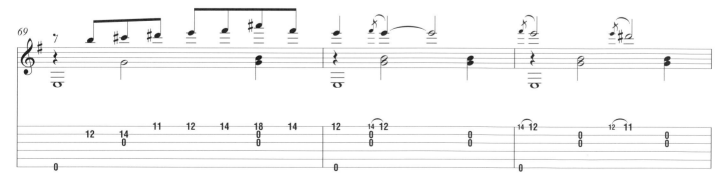

Sur la langue

Gymnopédie No. 1

Erik Satie
Arranged by Bridget Mermikides

Lent et douloureux

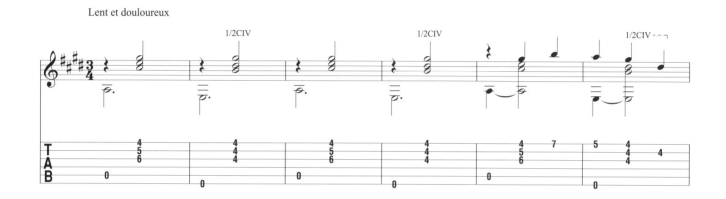

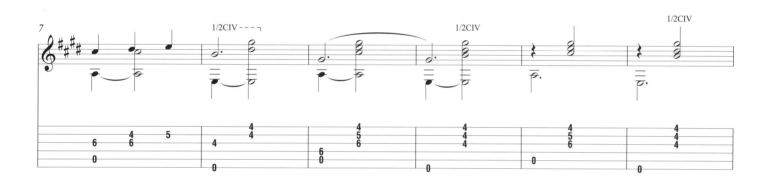

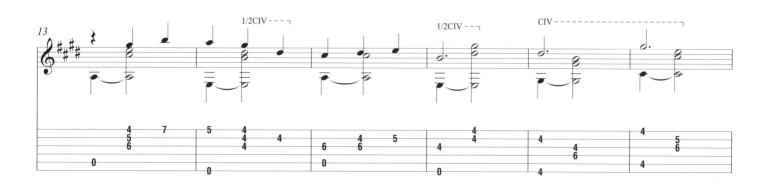

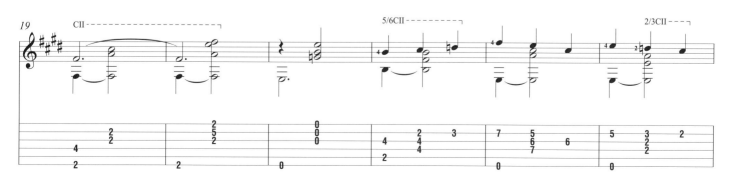

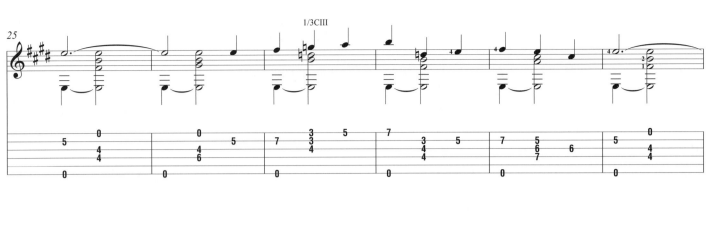

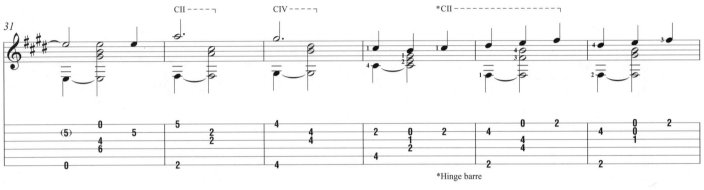

*Hinge barre

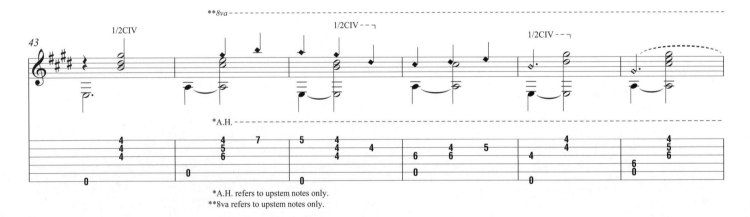

*A.H. refers to upstem notes only.
**8va refers to upstem notes only.

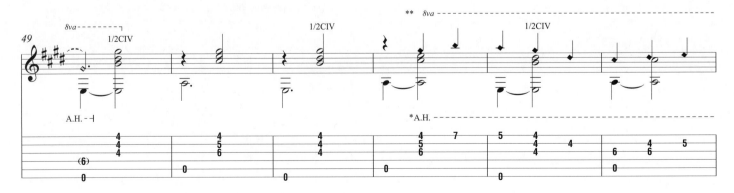

**Harm. refers to upstem note only.

Gymnopédie No. 3

Erik Satie
Arranged by Bridget Mermikides

Ave Maria

Franz Schubert
Arranged by Bridget Mermikides

let ring throughout

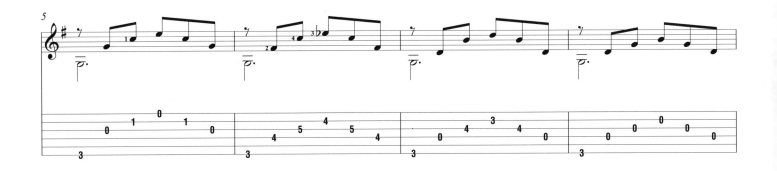

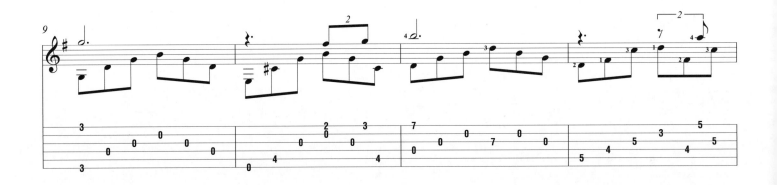

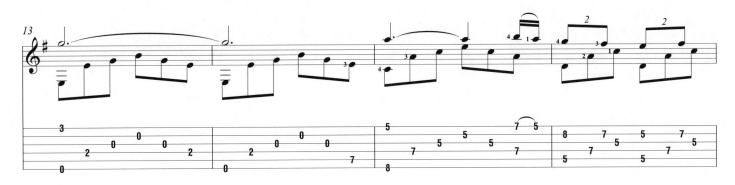

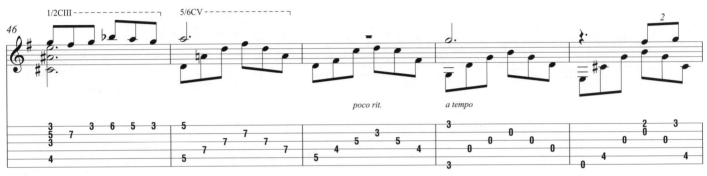

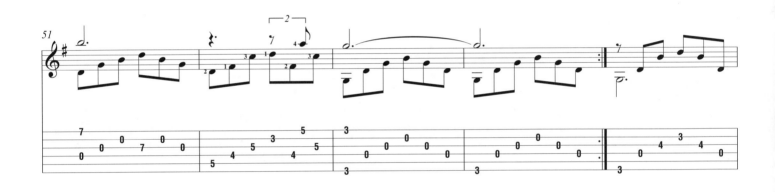

Traümerei

Robert Schumann
Arranged by Bridget Mermikides

Tuning:
(low to high) C-G-D-G-B-E

Dance of the Sugar Plum Fairy

Pyotr Ilyich Tchaikovsky
Arranged by Bridget Mermikides

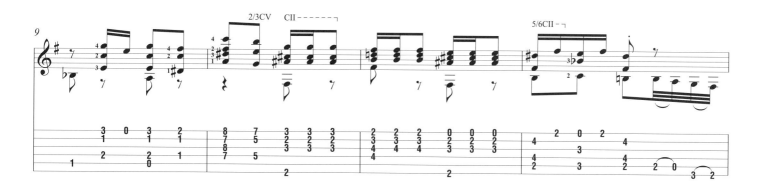

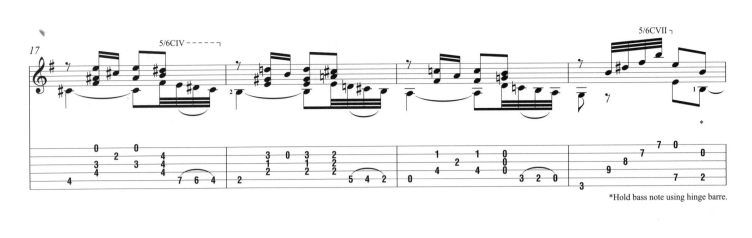

5/6CIV - - - - - -

5/6CVII

*Hold bass note using hinge barre.

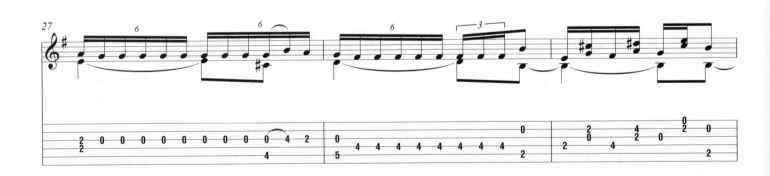

1/3CVII

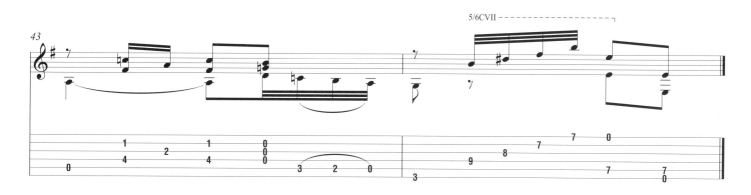

La Forza del Destino

Giuseppe Verdi
Arranged by Bridget Mermikides

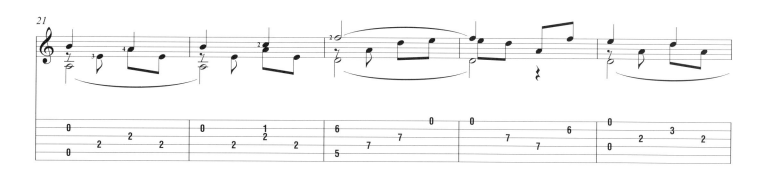

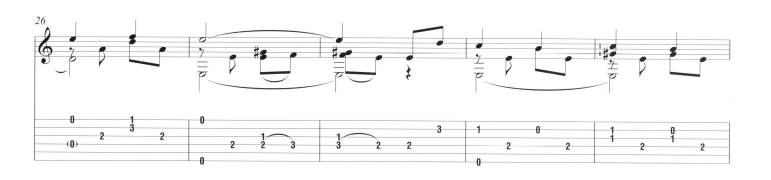

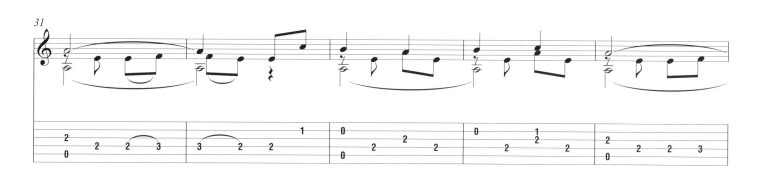

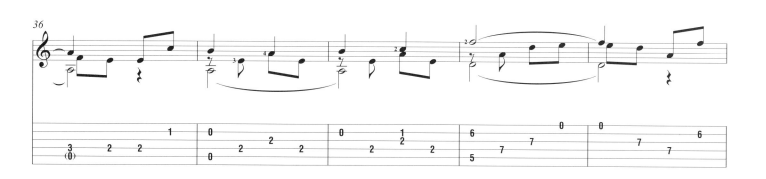

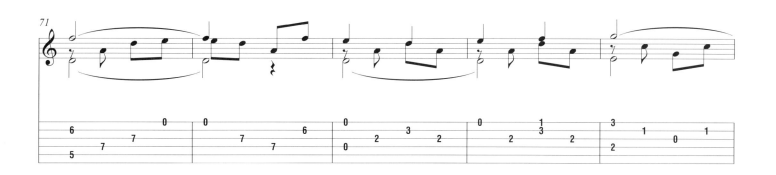

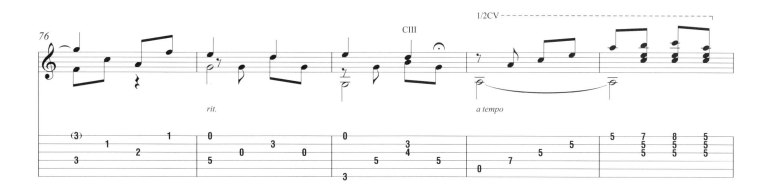

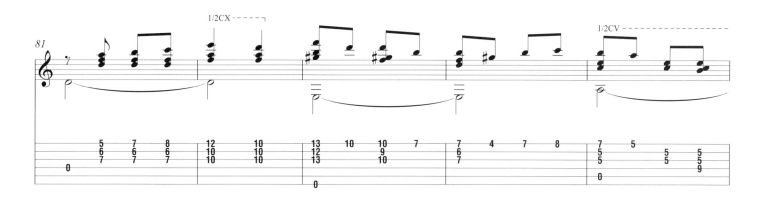

Ride of the Valkyries

Richard Wagner
Arranged by Bridget Mermikides

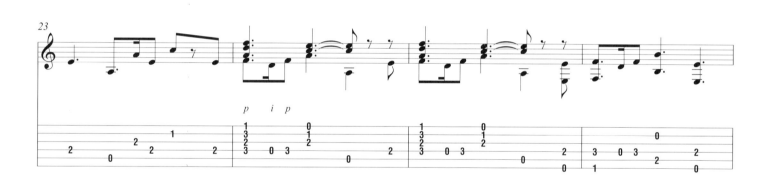

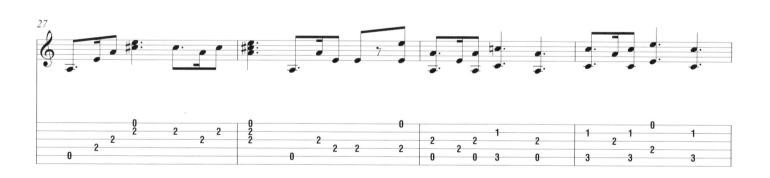

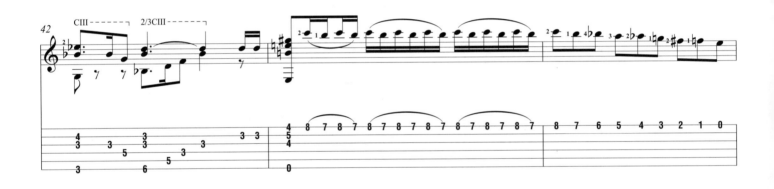

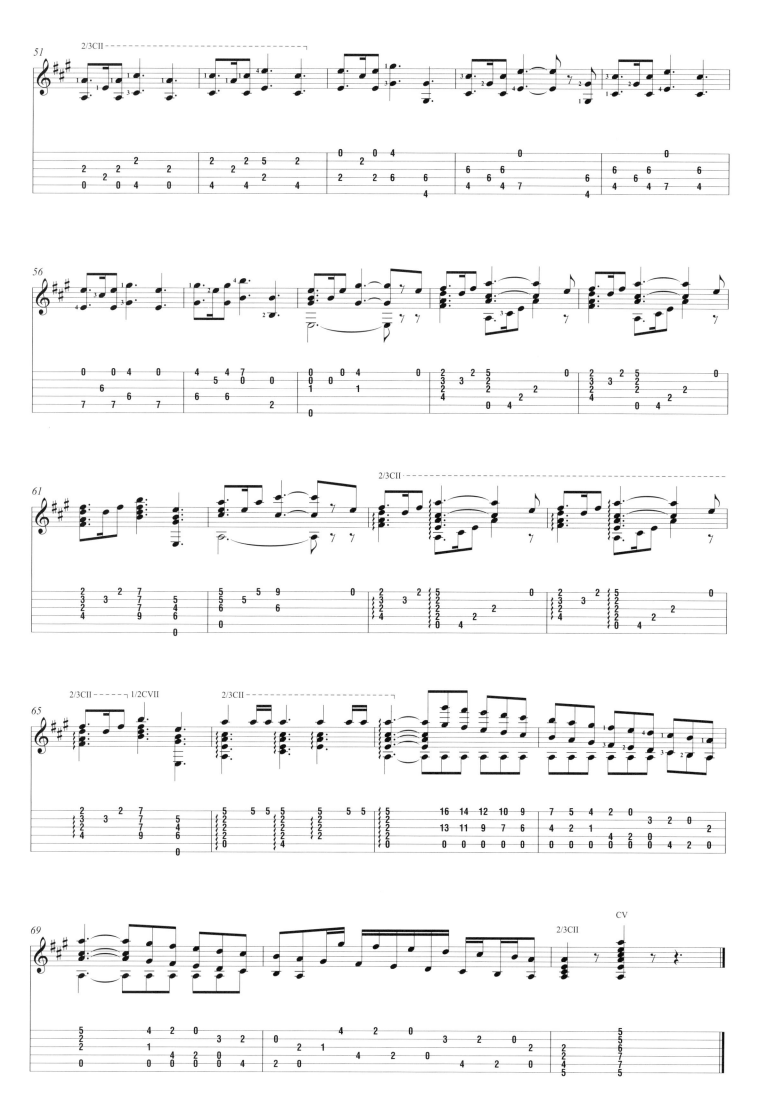

About the Author

Bridget Mermikides (formerly Upson) grew up in a family of classical musicians in the Lake District of England and studied the cello at age 6. Upon hearing a John Williams recording at age 13, she became instantly and irrecoverably smitten with the classical guitar and has since devoted her life to the instrument.

A graduate of the Royal Academy of Music (where she received tuition from John Williams and Julian Bream), Bridget now teaches, performs as a soloist and ensemble player and writes a monthly classical guitar column for Guitar Techniques magazine. Bridget lives in London with her husband and baby daughter.

www.bridgetmermikides.com

CLASSICAL GUITAR

THE BEATLES FOR CLASSICAL GUITAR

Includes 20 solos from big Beatles hits arranged for classical guitar, complete with left-hand and right-hand fingering. Songs include: All My Loving • And I Love Her • Can't Buy Me Love • Fool on the Hill • From a Window • Hey Jude • If I Fell • Let It Be • Michelle • Norwegian Wood • Obla Di • Ticket to Ride • Yesterday • and more. Features arrangements and an introduction by Joe Washington, as well as his helpful hints on classical technique and detailed notes on how to play each song. The book also covers parts and specifications of the classical guitar, tuning, and Joe's "Strata System" – an easy-reading system applied to chord diagrams.
00699237 Classical Guitar $19.99

CZERNY FOR GUITAR

INCLUDES TAB

12 SCALE STUDIES FOR CLASSICAL GUITAR
by David Patterson

Adapted from Carl Czerny's *School of Velocity, Op. 299* for piano, this lesson book explores 12 keys with 12 different approaches or "treatments." You will explore a variety of articulations, ranges and technical perspectives as you learn each key. These arrangements will not only improve your ability to play scales fluently, but will also develop your ears, knowledge of the fingerboard, reading abilities, strength and endurance. In standard notation and tablature.
00701248 ....$9.99

MATTEO CARCASSI – 25 MELODIC AND PROGRESSIVE STUDIES, OP. 60

arr. Paul Henry

One of Carcassi's (1792-1853) most famous collections of classical guitar music – indispensable for the modern guitarist's musical and technical development. Performed by Paul Henry. 49-minute audio accompaniment.
00696506 Book/Online Audio $17.99

CLASSICAL & FINGERSTYLE GUITAR TECHNIQUES

INCLUDES TAB

by David Oakes • Musicians Institute

This Master Class is aimed at any electric or acoustic guitarist who wants a quick, thorough grounding in the essentials of classical and fingerstyle technique. Topics covered include: arpeggios and scales, free stroke and rest stroke, P-i scale technique, three-to-a-string patterns, natural and artificial harmonics, tremolo and rasgueado, and more. The book includes 12 intensive lessons for right and left hand in standard notation & tab, and the audio features 92 solo acoustic tracks.
00695171 Book/Online Audio $17.99

CLASSICAL GUITAR CHRISTMAS COLLECTION

INCLUDES TAB

Includes classical guitar arrangements in standard notation and tablature for more than two dozen beloved carols: Angels We Have Heard on High • Auld Lang Syne • Ave Maria • Away in a Manger • Canon in D • The First Noel • God Rest Ye Merry, Gentlemen • Hark! the Herald Angels Sing • I Saw Three Ships • Jesu, Joy of Man's Desiring • Joy to the World • O Christmas Tree • O Holy Night • Silent Night • What Child Is This? • and more.
00699493 Guitar Solo $10.99

CLASSICAL GUITAR WEDDING

INCLUDES TAB

Perfect for players hired to perform for someone's big day, this songbook features 16 classsical wedding favorites arranged for solo guitar in standard notation and tablature. Includes: Air on the G String • Ave Maria • Bridal Chorus • Canon in D • Jesu, Joy of Man's Desiring • Minuet • Sheep May Safely Graze • Wedding March • and more.
00699563 Solo Guitar with Tab..............................$12.99

CLASSICAL MASTERPIECES FOR GUITAR

INCLUDES TAB

27 works by Bach, Beethoven, Handel, Mendelssohn, Mozart and more transcribed with standard notation and tablature. Now anyone can enjoy classical material regardless of their guitar background. Also features stay-open binding.
00699312 ....$14.99

MASTERWORKS FOR GUITAR

INCLUDES TAB

Over 60 Favorites from Four Centuries
World's Great Classical Music

Dozens of classical masterpieces: Allemande • Bourree • Canon in D • Jesu, Joy of Man's Desiring • Lagrima • Malaguena • Mazurka • Piano Sonata No. 14 in C# Minor (Moonlight) Op. 27 No. 2 First Movement Theme • Ode to Joy • Prelude No. I (Well-Tempered Clavier).
00699503 ....$19.99

A MODERN APPROACH TO CLASSICAL GUITAR

by Charles Duncan

This multi-volume method was developed to allow students to study the art of classical guitar within a new, more contemporary framework. For private, class or self-instruction. Book One incorporates chord frames and symbols, as well as a recording to assist in tuning and to provide accompaniments for at-home practice. Book One also introduces beginning fingerboard technique and music theory. Book Two and Three build upon the techniques learned in Book One.
00695114 Book 1 – Book Only...............................$6.99
00695113 Book 1 – Book/Online Audio................$10.99
00695116 Book 2 – Book Only...............................$6.99
00695115 Book 2 – Book/Online Audio................$10.99
00699202 Book 3 – Book Only...............................$9.99
00695117 Book 3 – Book/Online Audio................$12.99
00695119 Composite Book/CD Pack....................$29.99

ANDRES SEGOVIA – 20 STUDIES FOR GUITAR

Sor/Segovia

20 studies for the classical guitar written by Beethoven's contemporary, Fernando Sor, revised, edited and fingered by the great classical guitarist Andres Segovia. These essential repertoire pieces continue to be used by teachers and students to build solid classical technique. Features 50-minute demonstration audio.
00695012 Book/Online Audio $19.99
00006363 Book Only..$7.99

THE FRANCISCO COLLECTION TARREGA

INCLUDES TAB

edited and performed by Paul Henry

Considered the father of modern classical guitar, Francisco Tárrega revolutionized guitar technique and composed a wealth of music that will be a cornerstone of classical guitar repertoire for centuries to come. This unique book/audio pack features 14 of his most outstanding pieces in standard notation and tab, edited and performed by virtuoso Paul Henry. Includes: Adelita • Capricho Árabe • Estudio Brillante • Grand Jota • Lágrima • Malagueña • María • Recuerdos de la Alhambra • Tango • and more, plus bios of Tárrega and Henry.
00698993 Book/Online Audio $19.99

THE PUBLICATIONS OF
CHRISTOPHER PARKENING

CHRISTOPHER PARKENING – DUETS AND CONCERTOS

Throughout his career, Christopher Parkening has had the opportunity to perform with many of the world's leading artists and orchestras, and this folio contains many selections from those collaborations. All of the pieces included here have been edited and fingered for the guitar by Christopher Parkening himself.

00690938...$24.99

THE CHRISTOPHER PARKENING GUITAR METHOD, VOL. 1 – REVISED

in collaboration with
Jack Marshall and David Brandon

Learn the art of the classical guitar with this premier method for beginners by one of the world's preeminent virtuosos and the recognized heir to the legacy of Andrés Segovia. Learn basic classical guitar technique by playing beautiful pieces of music, including over 50 classical pieces, 26 exercises, and 14 duets. Includes notes in the first position, how to hold the guitar, tuning, right and left hand technique, arpeggios, tone production, placement of fingers and nails, flats, naturals, key signatures, the bar, and more. Also includes many helpful photos and illustrations, plus sections on the history of the classical guitar, selecting a guitar, guitar care, and more.

00695228 Book..$12.99
00696023 Book/Online Audio $19.99

THE CHRISTOPHER PARKENING GUITAR METHOD, VOL. 2

Intermediate to Upper-Intermediate Level

Continues where Vol. 1 leaves off. Teaches: all notes in the upper position; tone production; advanced techniques such as tremolo, harmonics, vibrato, pizzicato and slurs; practice tips; stylistic interpretation; and more. The first half of the book deals primarily with technique, while the second half of the book applies the technique with repertoire pieces. As a special bonus, this book includes 32 previously unpublished Parkening edition pieces by composers including Dowland, Bach, Scarlatti, Sor, Tarrega and other, plus three duets for two guitars.

00695229 Book..$12.99
00696024 Book/Online Audio $19.99

PARKENING AND THE GUITAR – VOL. 1

Music of Two Centuries:
Popular New Transcriptions for Guitar
Virtuoso Music for Guitar

Ten transcriptions for solo guitar of beautiful music from many periods and styles, edited and fingered by Christopher Parkening. All pieces are suitable for performance by the advanced guitarist. Ten selections: Afro-Cuban Lullaby • Empress of the Pagodes (Ravel) • Menuet (Ravel) • Minuet in D (Handel) • Passacaille (Weiss) • Pastourelle (Poulenc) • Pavane for a Dead Princess (Ravel) • Pavane for a Sleeping Beauty (Ravel) • Preambulo (Scarlatti-Ponce) • Sarabande (Handel).

00699105..$9.95

PARKENING AND THE GUITAR – VOL. 2

Music of Two Centuries:
Popular New Transcriptions for Guitar
Virtuoso Music for Guitar

Nine more selections for the advanced guitarist: Clair de Lune (Debussy) • Giga (Visée) • The Girl with the Flaxen Hair (Debussy) • Gymnopedie Nos. I-III (Satie) • The Little Shepherd (Debussy) • The Mysterious Barricades (Couperin) • Sarabande (Debussy).

00699106..$9.95

CHRISTOPHER PARKENING – ROMANZA

Virtuoso Music for Guitar

Three wonderful transcriptions edited and fingered by Parkening: Catalonian Song • Rumores de la Caleta • Romance.

00699103...$9.99

CHRISTOPHER PARKENING – SACRED MUSIC FOR THE GUITAR, VOL. 1

Seven inspirational arrangements, transcriptions and compositions covering traditional Christian melodies from several centuries. These selections appear on the Parkening album Sacred Music for the Guitar. Includes: Präludium (Bach) • Our Great Savior • God of Grace and God of Glory (2 guitars) • Brethren, We Have Met to Worship • Deep River • Jesus, We Want to Meet • Evening Prayer.

00699095...$12.99

CHRISTOPHER PARKENING – SACRED MUSIC FOR THE GUITAR, VOL. 2

Seven more selections from the album *Sacred Music for the Guitar:* Hymn of Christian Joy (guitar and harpsichord) • Simple Gifts • Fairest Lord Jesus • Stir Thy Church, O God Our Father • All Creatures of Our God and King • Glorious Things of Thee Are Spoken • Praise Ye the Lord (2 guitars).

00699100...$12.99

CHRISTOPHER PARKENING – SOLO PIECES

Sixteen transcriptions for solo guitar edited and fingered by Parkening, including: Allegro • Danza • Fugue • Galliard • I Stand at the Threshold • Prelude • Sonata in D • Suite Española • Suite in D Minor • and more.

00690939...$19.99

PARKENING PLAYS BACH

Virtuoso Music for Guitar

Nine transcriptions edited and fingered by Parkening: Preludes I, VI & IX • Gavottes I & II • Jesu, Joy of Man's Desiring • Sheep May Safely Graze • Wachet Auf, Ruft Uns Die Stemme • Be Thou with Me • Sleepers Awake (2 guitars).

00699104...$9.95

CHRISTOPHER PARKENING – VIRTUOSO PERFORMANCES

This DVD features performances and career highlights from classical guitar virtuoso Christopher Parkening (filmed in 1971, 1973, 1998 and 2003). Viewers can watch feature titles in their entirety or select individual songs. As a bonus, there is archival footage of Andrés Segovia performing in studio, circa 1950. The DVD also includes an informational booklet. 95 minutes.

00320506 DVD $24.99

HAL•LEONARD®

www.halleonard.com

Prices, contents and availability subject to change without notice.

FINGERPICKING GUITAR BOOKS

Hone your fingerpicking skills with these great songbooks featuring solo guitar arrangements in standard notation and tablature. The arrangements in these books are carefully written for intermediate-level guitarists. Each song combines melody and harmony in one superb guitar fingerpicking arrangement. Each book also includes an introduction to basic fingerstyle guitar.

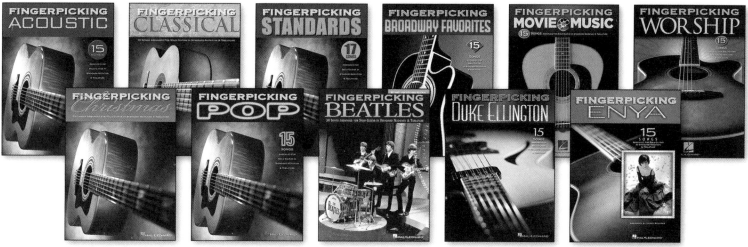

FINGERPICKING ACOUSTIC
00699614...$14.99

FINGERPICKING ACOUSTIC CLASSICS
00160211...$14.99

FINGERPICKING ACOUSTIC HITS
00160202...$12.99

FINGERPICKING ACOUSTIC ROCK
00699764...$12.99

FINGERPICKING BALLADS
00699717...$12.99

FINGERPICKING BEATLES
00699049...$19.99

FINGERPICKING BEETHOVEN
00702390...$8.99

FINGERPICKING BLUES
00701277 ....$9.99

FINGERPICKING BROADWAY FAVORITES
00699843...$9.99

FINGERPICKING BROADWAY HITS
00699838...$7.99

FINGERPICKING CELTIC FOLK
00701148...$10.99

FINGERPICKING CHILDREN'S SONGS
00699712...$9.99

FINGERPICKING CHRISTIAN
00701076 ....$7.99

FINGERPICKING CHRISTMAS
00699599...$9.99

FINGERPICKING CHRISTMAS CLASSICS
00701695...$7.99

FINGERPICKING CHRISTMAS SONGS
00171333...$9.99

FINGERPICKING CLASSICAL
00699620...$10.99

FINGERPICKING COUNTRY
00699687...$10.99

FINGERPICKING DISNEY
00699711...$15.99

FINGERPICKING EARLY JAZZ STANDARDS
00276565 ....$12.99

FINGERPICKING DUKE ELLINGTON
00699845...$9.99

FINGERPICKING ENYA
00701161...$10.99

FINGERPICKING FILM SCORE MUSIC
00160143...$12.99

FINGERPICKING GOSPEL
00701059...$9.99

FINGERPICKING GUITAR BIBLE
00691040 ....$19.99

FINGERPICKING HIT SONGS
00160195...$12.99

FINGERPICKING HYMNS
00699688...$9.99

FINGERPICKING IRISH SONGS
00701965...$9.99

FINGERPICKING ITALIAN SONGS
00159778...$12.99

FINGERPICKING JAZZ FAVORITES
00699844...$9.99

FINGERPICKING JAZZ STANDARDS
00699840...$10.99

FINGERPICKING ELTON JOHN
00237495...$12.99

FINGERPICKING LATIN FAVORITES
00699842...$9.99

FINGERPICKING LATIN STANDARDS
00699837...$12.99

FINGERPICKING ANDREW LLOYD WEBBER
00699839...$14.99

FINGERPICKING LOVE SONGS
00699841...$12.99

FINGERPICKING LOVE STANDARDS
00699836 ....$9.99

FINGERPICKING LULLABYES
00701276...$9.99

FINGERPICKING MOVIE MUSIC
00699919...$10.99

FINGERPICKING MOZART
00699794...$9.99

FINGERPICKING POP
00699615...$12.99

FINGERPICKING POPULAR HITS
00139079...$12.99

FINGERPICKING PRAISE
00699714...$10.99

FINGERPICKING ROCK
00699716...$12.99

FINGERPICKING STANDARDS
00699613...$12.99

FINGERPICKING WEDDING
00699637...$9.99

FINGERPICKING WORSHIP
00700554...$10.99

FINGERPICKING NEIL YOUNG – GREATEST HITS
00700134...$14.99

FINGERPICKING YULETIDE
00699654...$9.99

HAL•LEONARD®

Visit Hal Leonard online at **www.halleonard.com**

Prices, contents and availability
subject to change without notice.

0619
279